MW00966856

SILENT SOUL

SILENT SOUL

The Miracles
and Mysteries of
Audrey Santo

ANTONIA FELIX

Thomas Dunne Books   St. Martin's Press   New York

For Lawrence

Contents

Linda Santo addresses a group of visitors in her family chapel. The sign on the altar reads, THANK YOU FOR NOT TOUCHING ANYTHING. JESUS & MARY WILL TOUCH YOU. *The large image of Our Lady of Guadeloupe on the left was the first object in the Santo home to exhibit the mysterious oil that now covers many religious statues and other articles in the chapel.* (DAYNA SMITH © 1998, *THE WASHINGTON POST.* REPRINTED WITH PERMISSION.)

Acknowledgments

One of the great pleasures of writing this book has been the opportunity to meet a wonderful group of people who were enormously helpful in the course of my research. First, my deep thanks go to the Quinlan family of Worcester, Massachusetts, for their tireless efforts and warm hospitality. I also thank those contributors whose identities have been withheld to protect their privacy; without your generous input, this book would not have been possible. My warm gratitude also goes to the many professionals who took the time to explore ideas with me, including Dr. Lionel Corbett, Dr. Thayer Greene, Dr. Marc Feldman, Reverend Audrey Schindler, and Monsignor Vincent Keane. Finally, I thank my husband, Stanford, for his honest and productive feedback, thought-provoking discussions, and loving support every step of the way.

Interviewer: Do you now believe in God?

Carl Jung: I don't need to believe. I know.

—*C. G. Jung Speaking:*
Interviews and Encounters

Introduction

I first heard the story of Audrey Santo on a *20/20* feature in the spring of 1999. This moving piece left me fascinated by the possibility that people were being healed in the presence of a severely disabled girl. Like many who watched that program, I was also touched by the determination of Audrey's mother, Linda, who faces her daughter's condition with tireless hope for a recovery and oversees her round-the-clock special needs with a cheerful, down-to-earth attitude. As I looked further into Audrey's story, I learned that she is surrounded by many supernatural phenomena, in addition to claims of physical healing, that are currently being investigated by the Catholic diocese in Worcester, Massachusetts. Not only are hundreds of people convinced that their physical cures are due to Audrey's intervention, they are experiencing a renewal of faith by witnessing the religious statues and images that mysteriously weep oil in the family chapel.

These inexplicable events have drawn thousands of people to Audrey's home, including me, once I decided that I would like to write about this enormously popular pilgrimage site in the heart of New England. Because of the current phase of the Church's investigation, it is no longer possible to view Audrey through a window in her bedroom wall, nor would anyone in the family permit me to interview them. I was able, however, to view Audrey at her annual "presentation" event at the local church in August 1999. Fifteen-year-old Audrey was brought in on a stretcher by ambulance and placed behind a large window in a back room. Thousands of us filed past her that day.

In the course of my research for this book, I also interviewed and read press reports about people who have traveled to the Santo home and claim either spiritual or physical healing from those visits. I viewed the television programs and videos that have been produced about Audrey Santo and consulted with priests, theologians, and others about the claims of her miraculous powers. Throughout this process I have approached the subject of Christian mysticism and its most exotic phenomena—similar to what is occurring in the Santo home—with an open mind. My own religious perspective embraces miraculous events, but not necessarily as gifts from a divine source that are portioned out to only a chosen few. The very fact that we wake up each morning; experience loving relationships; overcome personal obstacles; create businesses, art, and music; express kindness and care about one another is evidence to me of the miraculous nature of everyday life. When I hear about "extraordinary" miracles, I feel renewed curiosity about the mysteries, both physical and spiritual, that our technological society can't penetrate.

If the field of mind-body medicine continues to progress as it has over the past three decades, things that are considered miraculous today may one day be explained by a new understanding of the laws of nature. Details about the mind-body connection that were considered fringe or inexplicable ten years ago, for example, are now scientifically proved and universally accepted by the medical community. What appears to be supernatural or spiritually unique is, perhaps, an extension of natural laws that we have not yet discovered. New revelations in physics have drastically transformed our ideas about the physical world, which has come to resemble more a play of energy that blinks in and out of existence than a collection of tiny building blocks. This opens the door to the idea that the unseen, energetic world—including the electromagnetic field of the human body—affects the outer world.

The outer world surrounding Audrey Santo is home to many strange occurrences. Is it possible that a person immersed in religious devotion has the power to produce physical manifestations of that devotion in his or her body or environment? Catholic Church history contains many stories of saints who experienced unusual effects of mysticism such as the stigmata and other physical conditions associated with the sufferings of Christ. *Attributing such phenomena to the mind-body connection revealed by medical science does not have to negate the religious nature of the experience*—rather, such an exploration may lead to the discovery of every human being's natural capacity for spiritual experience. This is one of the ideas that has captivated me throughout my study of Audrey Santo, her religious inheritance, and the supernatural events that surround her. Looking deeper into the power of the human mind is only one aspect of this inquiry, however, because scientific and psychological methods can go only so far in understanding something as purely subjective as spiritual experience. Psychiatrist Carl Jung, who devoted much study to the religious aspect of humanity and the spiritual substructure shared by all people, admitted that "the realities of faith lie outside the realm of psychology." Jung's work ushered in a new school of thought regarding human spirituality and provides a new context in which to look at apparitions of the Blessed Virgin Mary and other mystical phenomena that have become so prevalent in recent years. This is one of the views pertaining to the supernatural events surrounding Audrey Santo that is explored in this book.

Regardless of religious, philosophical, or scientific explanation, the positive and sometimes life-changing experiences of many people who have come into contact with Audrey Santo are very real and significant to them. The experiences have enriched their spiritual lives, validated their belief in prayer, and ignited a new sense of awe toward the mystery of life and of God. They feel a larger capacity to love, which overflows into the lives of their families and friends and coworkers. By sharing my personal journey into the story of Audrey Santo, I hope that this narrative collection of established fact, miraculous claims, and theoretical ideas will perhaps bring something new and insightful to the reader's own adventures with miracles and meaning.

1.

Intensive Care

Miracles are happening and we don't have to go to Lourdes or Fátima or Guadalupe. It's right here in Worcester, Massachusetts.

—Sister Marguerite Patient

"At the end of June 1999, my cardiologist said to my wife, 'I usually don't say this, but I'm taking my hat off to you both; your husband's in remission.'"

Six months earlier Vinny B., a forty-four-year-old man from Worcester, Massachusetts, had received devastating news: lung cancer. "At first they thought he had Hodgkin's," said Vinny's wife, Peggy. "Then they diagnosed lung cancer. Third stage. One step away from fourth, the worst. We had no clue he was that sick. I knew in my heart what the outlook could have been, but I didn't let the doctor tell us that." Vinny immediately began chemotherapy and radiology treatments—and visits to a house on the west side of town where remarkable things were happening.

The Santo family had turned their garage into a small chapel, complete with an altar and dozens of religious statues and pictures. Thousands of people had come through the door in the past few years to witness amazing supernatural events and receive physical and spiritual healing. Sitting with his wife in the chapel, Vinny prayed the rosary and asked a young girl inside the house to pray for him. Fifteen-year-old Audrey Santo lay in her bedroom, out of sight but very much on the minds of everyone in the chapel. Paralyzed and confined to her bed, she was the focus of the mysterious things occurring throughout the home, in the chapel, and in the lives of those who visited her home. Vinny believes that Audrey heard his prayers and helped him survive. Not only did she help him beat his cancer, she enabled him to overcome the painful side effects of his chemotherapy treatments.

"I had neuropathy," said Vinny. "I was limping around, I couldn't walk very good. I looked like I was really broken down." Neuropathy, the nerve damage caused by chemotherapy, is often irreversible and must be treated with pain medication for the rest of the cancer survivor's life. "Vinny had neuropathy very bad in his right knee," said Peggy, "to the point that he couldn't walk ten feet without bending over. They were putting him on medication, but nothing was working. I'd take him to the lake with me for our usual run, and it would break my heart because he couldn't go very far. They told him to just learn to live with it." Then Peggy decided to use some of the mysterious oil she had received at Audrey Santo's chapel. Every day oil appears on the statues and pictures in the chapel in such a constant flow that small plastic cups are attached to the objects to collect it. Cotton balls are dipped in the oil, placed in plastic bags, and given to visitors free of charge.

Peggy rubbed this oil on Vinny's chest and on his aching

legs and knees. After a few days he woke up one morning without a trace of pain. "We went in for a follow-up appointment, and Vinny told our nurse practitioner that the pain in his legs was gone," said Peggy. "The nurse told us that was miraculous because it just doesn't *do* that, it's a chronic ailment. The neuropathy didn't gradually slow down; it was just gone. We expected it to come back because he had more chemo to go through, but he hasn't had a recurrence of it at all." A few months after he was cured of cancer, Vinny returned to Audrey's chapel and plans to visit it every now and then. "Now that I'm on the right road to recovery and things are cool, I don't want to forget," he said. "I think there was more to my healing than my medical treatment. I felt like visiting the chapel was helping me somehow. We knew that through the power of thousands of people who were going to her that her power was strong, and I just felt that maybe she would hear me. It was a hopeful feeling, like faith. I think she's a saint for our time. She's going to be a saint, I know she is. There are just too many good endings in the stories of people who have gone to her."

The list of good endings includes a woman cured of ovarian cancer, a teenager miraculously recovered from a motorcycle accident, and a woman with multiple sclerosis free of pain for the first time in fifteen years. The chronicle of inexplicable events in Audrey's home includes statues and images that weep blood and oil; chalices and other articles that fill with oil; statues that shift position; and Communion hosts that manifest bloodstains. Even more mysterious are the phenomena happening to Audrey herself: she has reportedly taken on some of the symptoms of the people who visit or petition to her, and she repeatedly receives marks on her body and endures distress that resembles the stigmata—the emotional and physical experience of Christ's suffering in the last hours of his life.

The story of Audrey Santo is a tale of remarkable events and claims that have rekindled the Christian faith of thousands of people, both laypeople and priests. What began with a tragic accident has become a growing source of inspiration for people who are looking for everything from physical healing to proof of the existence of God. At the very heart of this mystery is Audrey herself, a teenage girl who has been paralyzed and in a semicomatose state since the age of three. Is she able to hear and comprehend the people around her? Does she really respond through expressions in her eyes and by squeezing your hand, or is her family misinterpreting random gestures because they so desperately want to believe Audrey is consciously with them? Did she at some point make a decision to become a "victim soul," a person who willingly takes on the suffering of others to help in the redemption of humanity?

These questions have been answered by Audrey's family, caregivers, and some of the clergy who are close to them, and are addressed throughout this book. They are also important concerns of the Catholic diocese in Worcester, which has been studying Audrey Santo closely. The Catholic Church is extremely careful about investigating claims of healing and supernatural events such as those occurring around Audrey Santo, and it has a long tradition of healthy skepticism and rigorous research.

Audrey's fateful accident and the miraculous claims surrounding her have been reported in newspapers from Seattle to Dublin and on television programs from *20/20, 48 Hours,* and *Unsolved Mysteries* to British TV shows such as *The Miracle Police.* It is a story that intrigues everyone who hears it, moving many of them to contemplate the possibility that miracles are alive and well in the new millennium.

The story begins on a Sunday morning in August 1987. Audrey's elder sister, sixteen-year-old Jennifer, picked up Audrey at their grandparents' house (where she had spent the night), so that the family could go to church together. Grandma and Grandpa Nader lived just a mile and a half away, and Audrey loved to visit them; she and her grandmother were especially close. Tiny, blue-eyed, auburn-haired Audrey had a sparkling personality that endeared her to everyone she met. Her constant companion was the family's German shepherd, Sting, who would pick her up by the seat of her pants and carry her around. In the family's eyes Audrey had a special spark, and her parents described her as "a handful." On that morning, however, the usually vivacious and chatty Audrey was quiet as she slipped into the backseat of the car. "That's very unusual for Audrey," recalled Jennifer. "Audrey's never quiet. She always has something to say." The little girl didn't say a word all the way home, much to the amazement of her sister. Looking back, Jennifer thought that Audrey sensed that it was going to be a different sort of day. "It was like she knew something was going to happen," she said.[1]

After Audrey and Jennifer got home, they went with their mother and two brothers, thirteen-year-old Matthew and four-year-old Stephen, to Mass at Christ the King Church.

Audrey's father, Stephen, was still pulling a double shift at Reed Plastics in the nearby town of Holden. After church the family had lunch at a diner, stopped in a toy shop, and were home by ten A.M. The two preschoolers, Stephen and Audrey, were outside playing together in front of the house just before eleven A.M. A few minutes later little Stephen came inside by himself, and Linda realized she was standing in the house with three of her children—but the youngest was not with them. "I looked at all three of them and I said, 'All my kids are here, where's my baby?'"[2]

Matthew quickly looked out a front window and didn't see her. Then they all rushed to the back door that led out to the deck and the backyard. From the deck they were horrified to see Audrey floating facedown in the aboveground swimming pool. The water in the sixteen-by-thirty-two-foot pool was four feet deep, and the pool was situated about ten feet from the deck. According to Detective Joseph Genduso, who investigated the accident, a ladder leading to the pool was pulled down. He said that the ladder was too large and out of reach for a child Audrey's size to move.[3] Matthew leaped from the deck into the pool, fully clothed, and pulled his baby sister out of the water. As Audrey lay on the raised platform that encircled the pool, her sister sprang into action. Jennifer, who had been trained in CPR about two years earlier, began mouth-to-mouth resuscitation. "All I was thinking was 'Audrey, breathe. Audrey, open up your eyes,'" said Jennifer. "It was so unbelievable."[4] A next-door neighbor, Mark Massey, rushed to Audrey's side and began chest compressions.

Linda called 911, and fortunately an ambulance happened

to be in that part of town and arrived within two minutes of receiving the call from the dispatcher. A second ambulance was also sent to their home at 1 Rockwood Avenue and pulled up to the house shortly afterward. By calling out two ambulances, the dispatchers hoped that two paramedic teams would be able to revive the child. "They said it was a three-year-old girl who wasn't breathing," said one of the paramedics, Lance Jorritsma. "Many hands make light work. It would be a lot easier for four people."[5] The first emergency team on the scene found Audrey very blue, with no pulse. Her eyes were fixed and dilated. One of the paramedics, John Lynch, took over the CPR that Jennifer and her neighbor had begun, taking Audrey in his arms and breathing into her mouth while giving her light chest compressions. Then his partner took over pressing on Audrey's chest while Lynch placed an endotracheal tube down the girl's windpipe in order to feed pure oxygen directly into her lungs. They strapped Audrey to a stretcher and placed her in the ambulance, feeding her oxygen and rhythmically pumping her heart the entire time. With each press on Audrey's chest, they hoped to send blood to her brain. Even though the girl had drowned, there was still a chance she could be revived; the more oxygen she received, the better her chances of not suffering permanent brain damage.

The police worked quickly to set up roadblocks along the ambulance's route to Worcester City Hospital and gave an escort from door to door. Because the paramedics were performing CPR, the ambulance was not able to travel any faster than thirty-five miles per hour, and the police escort allowed it to pass through every intersection without stopping. Inside, the paramedics hooked up Audrey to a heart monitor, and the readings were extremely weak. Ultimately the medical reports stated that she went into cardiac arrest in the ambulance. In radio contact with the hospital, the paramedics were instructed to give Audrey epinephrine and atropine to stimulate her heart. By the time they reached the emergency room, however, there was still no heartbeat.

Worcester City Hospital was close, and just seventeen minutes after the paramedics first arrived at Audrey's side, she was inside the emergency room. The medical team was able to get Audrey's heart beating, but she was still unconscious when they transferred her to UMass Memorial Medical Center about ten miles away. In the midst of all the hysteria, Linda and her children were questioned about how long Audrey had been in the pool. Although it was hard to reconstruct the exact timing of that morning, they believed she may have been in the water for five to fifteen minutes. All the medical staff, from the paramedics to the emergency-room doctors, were hoping that Audrey's mammalian diving reflex had kicked in. This reflex, also known as cold water shock, allows oxygen to be concentrated in the vital organs, primarily the heart and brain. The diving reflex is thought to be triggered by nerves in the forehead and around the nose when the face is immersed in water colder than seventy degrees. Audrey's skin was very blue when she was pulled from the pool, but no one could determine exactly how long she had been deprived of oxygen. The diving reflex is stronger in children than in adults, and everyone hoped for the best. "It's just a matter of waiting to see what happens at this time to see if the child has full neurological recovery," said emergency-room doctor Richard Larson the day after the accident.[6]

Even though Audrey had been transferred to the highly equipped pediatric intensive care unit at the UMass Medical Center, she was still in critical condition and her prognosis was not good. She had survived at all only because of the quick response of her sister in starting CPR. "Obviously, it was the cardiopulmonary resuscitation which saved her life and without that she would not be alive today," said Dr. Alison Anderson, one of Audrey's pediatricians in the intensive care unit. She added that doctors are adamant about trying to have "as many people certified in cardiopulmonary resuscitation or basic life support as possible, because even young people can save other people's lives."[7]

The doctors had given the three-year-old various drugs in an effort to protect her oxygen-deprived brain from further damage and to give it a chance to recover. The Santo family believes that the treatment Audrey received at the UMass Medical Center in the first two days of her stay actually hurt more than helped her. Years later, standing before a group of people gathered in her home chapel, Linda explained that "they overdosed her with drugs and they put her in a coma."[8]

Numb from shock and exhausted from the terrifying events of the past few hours, the Santo family received another devastating blow at the hospital that first evening. Audrey's accident and hospitalization had already ignited a flurry of local radio and television news stories, and the media were pressing the hospital for information. The administration set up a press conference, without notifying the family, and went on the air with a strong message about the Santos' neglect in not preventing the pool accident. That evening Linda, Stephen, and their children listened to the first implications that Audrey should have been watched more closely. A string of news reports repeated the accusation for weeks. In October, for example, Dr. Anderson stated in the local newspaper that drowning is the second leading cause of accidental death of children and urged parents to take every precaution against such incidents. "The most important risk factor is an unsupervised toddler," she said. "If we can just use this to encourage parents to keep a close watch of their child."[9] These ongoing articles were impossible to ignore, and Linda and her family were very hurt by them. "There is no way one of my kids was out of my sight for fifteen minutes," Linda firmly told the local newspaper. "That's why they call it an accident."[10]

After a few days the Santos were given a glimmer of hope. Audrey opened her eyes. It was a blank stare with no movement, but it was something—and certainly enough to refresh their optimism that she would recover. The medical staff was not encouraged, however, and after Audrey had been in intensive care for seven days, they suggested that the family consider taking her off the ventilator and feeding tube. The family refused. "They were telling me she wasn't going to make it," said Linda. "If she made it, maybe two years, she'd be a vegetable. It was probably the most hopeless place I'd ever been in."[11]

As she lay in the hospital week after week, Audrey continued to open her eyes now and then. Tests proved that she was also somewhat sensitive to pain, which gave the Santos even more hope that Audrey was on her way back. But eventually the hospital staff decided it was time to move Audrey to a long-term care facility. They asked Linda where she would like to place Audrey once she was released from the hospital. The Department of Social Services had a list of nursing homes that were equipped to handle a patient who needed special medical equipment and round-the-clock care. Linda, however, had no intention of putting her daughter in another medical facility. In her opinion, much of Audrey's experience at the UMass Medical Center had done her more harm than good. She had been given drugs that damaged her brain. She had been surrounded by medical personnel who repeatedly stated that there was no hope. And a physical therapist had broken both of Audrey's tiny, fragile legs during a session—an injury that didn't get reported until the family asked that her severely swollen knees be X-rayed. Linda told the hospital staff that she was not going to place Audrey in a nursing home but, rather, in her arms. "My thought was," Linda said, "I'm not gonna let her die, and neither is God because she's gonna be home with us."[12] The doctors thought the idea ridiculous and told Linda that Audrey would be dead within two weeks if she was brought home. But Linda insisted, stood her ground, and told them that she knew where her daughter belonged. "She's my child," she told them. "She's going home."[13]

The decision was made, and in October 1987 the family went into high gear to prepare for Audrey's homecoming. They sold their two-story house and moved into Grandma Nader's one-story ranch-style house on South Flagg Street. Audrey would have a bedroom on the main floor that was big enough for her heart monitor, respirator, and other medical equipment and from which it would be easy to move her in and out of the house for her medical appointments. Friends of the family volunteered to upgrade the electrical system of the house so that it would have enough power to run Audrey's medical equipment. Finally, on Friday afternoon, November 13, 1987, Audrey was taken home in an ambulance after a farewell party at the hospital. The doctors did not send Audrey off with a prognosis for recovery, nor did they have any idea what to expect in the next week, month, or year. "There is no prognosis," said Linda the day after Audrey came home. "The doctors refuse to give one. At one point, they gave her no chance. Now they hope. We take it one step at a time."[14]

The family filed a lawsuit against the hospital, claiming that the drugs used were responsible for Audrey's comalike condition. The court dismissed the suit on the grounds that it lacked substance. Linda continues to blame the hospital, however, in very matter-of-fact terms when she speaks to people about the treatment Audrey received at the UMass Medical Center.

On that November weekend Audrey moved into the bedroom in which she has remained ever since. Her mother and grandmother covered the window with airy white curtains, outfitted the bed with lacy pillowcases, strung a garland of artificial flowers along the top of the curtain valence, and placed Audrey's stuffed animals throughout the room. Small and fragile, still recuperating from her broken legs, Audrey lay motionless in the bed as everyone in her family spoke to her and kissed her in an attempt to bring her out of her unresponsive state. This would be the routine from that day forward: giving Audrey as much attention as possible and never giving up hope that she would one day wake up. Linda Santo set up a caretaker schedule so that every member of the family would have bedside duty during some part of the day. "They love her to pieces," Linda said of her other children after Audrey had been home for two months. "They just look at it like, 'She's my baby sister and she is going to get better.' We're sure she'll recover, as unrealistic as that might seem. There has never been any doubt in my mind."[15] Eventually Linda found a source of funding for twenty-four-hour-a-day nursing care, and the family schedule was relaxed somewhat. The Santos' tireless and cheerful devotion to Audrey made a profound impression on the diocese's bishop, who began investigating the claims surrounding Audrey in early 1998. After the preliminary part of the investigation was completed, he said in a press conference that "the most striking evidence of the presence of God in the Santo home is seen in the dedication of the family to Audrey. Their constant respect for her dignity as a child of God is a poignant reminder that God touches our lives through the love and devotion of others."

Audrey Santo continued to be news in her hometown of Worcester, the second-largest city in New England (with a population of about 170,000), and her story spread throughout the nation. The *Worcester Telegram & Gazette* ran regular updates on her condition after she returned home from the hospital. Churches and synagogues remembered Audrey in their prayers and organized bake sales to help the family pay for some of Audrey's care. A benefit, featuring music hosted by a popular Boston disc jockey, was organized at a Knights of Columbus hall. Raffle tickets were sold by schools, colleges, church groups, and small businesses from Worcester, and surrounding towns sent donations to the family. Audrey had found a permanent place in the community's heart as a fighter, and everyone was rooting for her.

Hundreds of well-wishers had visited Audrey in the hospital, and these visits continued after she was brought home. People came to the house with gifts—such as religious statues brought from Lourdes, Medjugorje, and other pilgrimage sites—which quickly filled up her room and overflowed into the rest of the house. Visitors also brought their prayers, asking God to heal the paralyzed little girl who had somehow survived but still had far to go. Some even began to pray *to* Audrey, believing that in her silence she had a special relationship with Jesus that allowed her to bring their prayers to him. With this transition from praying for Audrey to praying to her, the people who visited the Santo home initiated a practice that was later addressed by Bishop Daniel P. Reilly of the Worcester diocese in his press conference in January 1999:

In the case of Audrey herself, more study is needed from medical and other professionals regarding her level of awareness and her ability to communicate with the people around her. This is critical to the basis of the claim of her ability to intercede with God. In the meantime, I urge continued prayers for Audrey and her family. But praying to Audrey is not acceptable in Catholic teaching.

According to the newsletter published by the Santo family, the practice of praying for Audrey's intercession continues, however. The November 1999 edition contained a prayer addressed to "wonderful little Audrey" that includes the line "I/We beg you to pray with us poor sinners for the grace and courage to bear whole-heartedly whatever cross God has chosen for us before the foundation of the world. . . . Your silence is more eloquent than a thousand words. . . . Amen." Although this prayer asks Audrey to pray with the practitioner, it is a prayer addressed *to* Audrey. As Bishop Reilly stated, the Catholic Church does not condone praying to anyone other than God the Father and those holy enough to intercede for humanity, such as the saints. The Catholic catechism explains that Jesus is "the only mediator" but that prayers may be sent to Mary, the mother of Jesus, because "when we pray to her, we are adhering with her to the plan of the Father, who sends his Son to save all men. Like the beloved disciple we welcome Jesus' mother into our homes, for she has become the mother of all the living." Likewise, Christians are invited to pray to the saints—holy people who live in heaven with God—because "when they entered into the joy of their Master, they were 'put in charge of many things.' Their intercession is their most exalted service to God's plan. We can and should ask them to intercede for us and for the whole world." This catechism defines prayer as "a vital and personal relationship with the living and true God" and one of the great mysteries of faith.[16]

Even though prayers to someone who is reportedly working miracles, like Audrey, are not officially sanctioned by the Catholic Church, this prohibition has not prevented faithful

Catholics and people of all faiths from voicing their prayers to her. For more than a decade, growing numbers of Catholics, Protestants, Jews, and those not affiliated with any organized religion have come to the Santo home to pray in their own way. For some, praying to Audrey is part of a personal recognition that God is working through her. By praying the rosary in the Santo chapel, Vinny B. and his wife felt a strong healing power that they believe derives from the special innocence and holiness of Audrey Santo. Sister Patient believes that the miraculous results she gains from using the oil from the Santo chapel places Audrey at the center of a sacred mystery that rivals Lourdes, Fátima, and Guadalupe. For many, contemplating Audrey's silence and physical suffering has ignited an inner spiritual flame that had lain dormant for a lifetime. Listening to volunteers tell stories of the miraculous cures attributed to Audrey and watching oil drip from statues of the Virgin Mary have given many visitors new faith that with God, anything is possible. Doctors, nurses, housewives, businessmen, priests, artists, teenagers—people of many faiths and all walks of life have found inspiration in the small Santo chapel. In the opinion of the volunteers and priests who have greeted thousands of pilgrims on South Flagg Street, Audrey's ability to bring people together in an atmosphere of love and compassion reveals perhaps her greatest power of all.

In addition to the prayers addressed to Audrey, there is another level of veneration paid her that is not well documented—if known at all—outside the Santos' immediate circle of family and friends: Audrey's ability to do more than intercede for others and bring prayers to Jesus. Linda Santo told me that Audrey, like God, knows people's hearts and that she "cuts people off" when she judges that their actions are not performed in a godly way. It was not clear whether she meant the person would be cut off from Audrey, from Jesus, or from God, but the implication was that Audrey has the power to alter one's spiritual connection in a profound way. Such claims of "cutting off" stand in stark contrast to the benevolent and nonjudgmental atmosphere generated in the family chapel and in the materials distributed about Audrey. Bishop Reilly has not yet commented on these claims; however, further statements are expected from him as his investigation into Audrey Santo continues.

What began as a terrifying accident on a warm Sunday morning has evolved into an event that draws people from throughout the world. By initiating an official investigation into the events occurring in the Santo home, Bishop Reilly has revealed that Audrey Santo's effect on the faithful warrants for a closer look. If he concludes that these events are worthy of further study, he will state his case to the Vatican, and the investigation will continue on a new level. (The Church's process of investigating this type of phenomena is discussed later.) No one knows how long Bishop Reilly will take in making this determination, as no time line has been set up to commission doctors, psychologists, and others. Some believe that these are the first steps toward sainthood for a girl with a divine mission to fulfill, a girl who made an early start on her mysterious journey to God.

Audrey Santo's drowning left her mute, paralyzed, and in a difficult-to-measure state of consciousness. After returning home from the hospital, she continued to be surrounded by

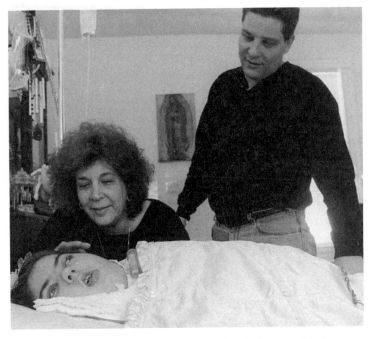

Linda and Stephen Santo at home with Audrey in January 2000. (PAULA FERAZZI SWIFT. REPRINTED WITH PERMISSION OF *THE WORCESTER TELEGRAM AND GAZETTE*.)

loving family and friends, but her life and that of each of her family members would never again be the same. As the family hoped and prayed for her recovery, events other than Audrey's physical healing began to unfold in the following months. These unusual happenings began after Linda and Audrey returned home after a dramatic trip in search of a miracle.

2.

A Mother's Mission

*When [Saint Veronica Giuliani (1660–1727)]
was just four years old, her mother Benedetta
was dying and entrusted each of her five daughters to one of the five wounds of Christ. . . . This
act on Benedetta's part proved to be prophetic,
for later on Veronica would become avidly
devoted to the Passion of our Lord, even to the
point of sharing His sufferings as she strove to
imitate His life.*

—from *They Bore the Wounds of Christ*[1]

Autumn 1999. Audrey is sixteen years old and continues to
baffle the doctors who treat her. Instead of spiraling into de-
cline and dying within weeks of being discharged from the
hospital, as some of the UMass Medical Center intensive care
staff had predicted, she has good vital signs and her bones
are strong enough to undergo regular physical-therapy sessions at home. These sessions include stretching out on a
large rubber ball, which prevents her muscles from contract-
ing permanently and keeps her joints flexible, and taking
warm whirlpool baths, which relax her muscles and calm her
breathing. Audrey's pediatrician, John Harding, M.D., is
amazed that she has never had bedsores in the thirteen years
she's been confined to bed. Her body has grown, although
her legs are slightly misshapen and her muscles are small
from disuse. The family has not released any official medical

reports but claims that Audrey's brain damage is not severe enough to affect the function of any vital organs.

According to Dr. Edward Kaye, a pediatric neurologist at the Children's Hospital of Philadelphia, who was Audrey's doctor for several years following the accident, her brain damage is substantial. Describing her injury, he said, "The cell death is about as bad as you can get and still be alive. Her EEGs are profoundly abnormal. She has brain stem activity, but very, very little above the brain stem." Regarding the girl's level of awareness, Dr. Kaye said, "There is little objective evidence that she can respond to external stimuli. There is no evidence to suggest that something gets through and gets processed. She is not brain-dead, because she has brain stem activity." He added, however, that "from a cognitive standpoint, she is dead."[2] Although the family and nurses are convinced that Audrey is aware of and reacts to them—and that she is becoming more aware all the time—Dr. Kaye believes this is just the hopeful interpretation that gives comfort to those who love Audrey. They have a desperate wish to make a connection with Audrey and feel that she is getting better, which can lead to interpreting reflexes or other subtle movements as signs of consciousness.

Coma specialist Dr. Ed Cooper has been working on a communication program involving hand signals and hopes Audrey will be able to use it one day. "If she can become consistent in the movements of her hands," he said in 1999, "such as down for 'yes' and up for 'no' or vice versa, then that would be meaningful, I think. But right now, it's inconsistent." He has also been treating Audrey with an experimental electrical-stimulation procedure to strengthen her muscles.[3] During the filming of the *20/20* feature "The Miracle of Audrey" in 1998, host Lynn Sherr took Audrey's hand, leaned slightly over the bed, and asked her to squeeze it. To Lynn's obvious pleasure and amazement, Audrey did. Later in the day she returned to Audrey's bedside and repeated the experiment. This time nothing happened.

Audrey cannot breathe or swallow on her own and requires life support in the form of a ventilator attached to a tracheostomy tube in her throat (for breathing) and a gastrostomy tube connected to her stomach (for feeding). Her inability to swallow also requires that her saliva be suctioned from her mouth continually, about every four minutes, day and night. Nurses and family members must also suction Audrey's tracheostomy tube every few hours to keep it clean and clear. Linda, Jennifer, and even young Stephen learned how to do the suctioning and take their turns at this and any other tasks, even after Linda found funding for a full-time nurse.

Audrey's nurses have been dedicated and meticulous in their service for the past thirteen years, and they have played a large part in Audrey's stable condition, lack of bedsores, and, according to the family, slow but ever developing return to awareness. Joanne Erickson, R.N., for example, has been working with Audrey since 1988 and is practically part of the family. The Santos consider her "Audrey's second mother" and affectionately refer to her as "the general." When Joanne first began working in the home, she didn't think there was much hope for a change in Audrey's condition. As the weeks, months, and years passed, however, she changed her mind. "I do really believe that someday she will speak and get up," she said in November 1999, "not in the sense that we [do], but she will function." Nurse Erickson has observed a very slow but positive course of change since she began working with Audrey eleven years ago. "She's bigger, she's gained weight and she's much taller," she said in an interview for the family newsletter. "She seems to have more responsiveness when you're talking to her and trying to get her to do things and she seems to be more alert. She seems to know more of what's going on."[4] Erickson said that when she comes into Audrey's room in the morning, the girl's eyes open wide and that at times Audrey fights with her just like any kid who doesn't want to do everything adults tell her to. "She wants to come off the vent. . . . If I try to keep her in one position she will go the opposite; she really challenges one."[5] Nurse Erickson explained that Audrey does have some movement: she can lift her head when she's on her stomach, move her left arm, turn her head slightly with stimulation to that side, and even flip herself over. These abilities, combined with the fact that Audrey's brain injury has never given her seizures, convince the nurse that there is an excellent chance that Audrey will keep getting better and eventually speak and get out of bed. Erickson's hope is bolstered by something that happened when she first began taking care of Audrey. The number seventeen came into her mind and has stayed with her, and she feels that it has some sort of meaning for Audrey's recovery. "If she'll be in this condition for seventeen years or she'll be healed when she's seventeen years old, I don't know," she said. "I still have that feeling. It could be 2017, who knows."

Other nurses have also spent months and even years at

Audrey's side, monitoring her vital signs, cleaning and suctioning her tubes, bathing her, moving her to prevent bedsores, helping the physical therapists and doctors, and growing close to the family. Linda has seen change flowing both ways between the nurses and Audrey, even in regard to the nurses' spiritual lives. In one case a nurse who worked for the family for a long period and developed a close relationship with Linda "was agnostic when she came—not when she left," said Linda.[6]

Since she first became a mother, Linda has always put the spiritual well-being of her children above everything else. All four times she became pregnant, she prayed to give birth to a saint. "I can give life, but only God can give eternal life," she explained.[7] With each pregnancy she made a special visit to her priest:

"Every time I got pregnant, I would call my spiritual director so that he would pray for me," said Linda. "Then we would meet at church so that he could consecrate the babies to the Immaculate Heart of Mary and the Sacred Heart of Jesus. Afterward, I'd say, 'You know what to pray for, Father,' and he'd always say, 'Pray for a saint!' "[8]

Raised in a devout Catholic home, Linda Santo has taken her religious faith seriously since childhood. She told writer Thomas Petrisko that she sought out spiritual direction at the age of nine.[9] In the Catholic tradition, spiritual direction is special guidance for those resolved to make progress in their spiritual life. Linda would always have someone to talk to about her faith and to help her live in accordance with the teachings of the Church. The person who acts as the spiritual director is often a priest and, according to the *Catholic Dictionary,* must be "someone who is specially qualified by education, experience, or personal sanctity to discern the will of God in the practice of Christian virtue."[10] Religion was an important part of family life for Linda's parents, Joseph and Patricia Nader, who gathered Linda and her three elder sisters together to pray the rosary at home every Friday night.

Linda's father was Lebanese and belonged to the Maronite Church, one of the Eastern rite churches. The Maronite Church descends from the ancient Christian Church of Antioch, whose first bishop was the apostle Peter. The first Maronite patriarch was Saint John Maron, who brought the Maronite community in Lebanon together into an organized church in the seventh century. The distinct traditions of this rite have remained intact despite centuries of invasions and persecution. The Maronite Church recognizes the Vatican and the pope as its primary spiritual authority. Next in leadership is the patriarch of Antioch, who lives near Beirut in Lebanon. The Maronite liturgy is spoken in Syriac, an ancient language very similar to Aramaic, which Jesus spoke. The Church has used the same liturgy—including a distinctive tradition of chants—since the fifth century, and this Service of the Holy Mysteries has preserved the unique identity of the Maronite rite. This tradition, like other Eastern churches, varies from the Roman Catholic rite in other significant ways as well, including allowing priests to marry. Maronite Catholicism spread throughout the world with the wave of emigration in the nineteenth century, and in addition to the one in Lebanon, there are now Maronite dioceses in Australia, the United States, Canada, Brazil, Cyprus, Egypt, and Syria. Of the 61 million Catholics in the United States, about 75,000 are Maronites.

The Eastern rite tradition is still close to Linda Santo's life in that one of her own family's spiritual directors is a married Eastern rite priest, Father Emmanuel Charles McCarthy. He is a Melkite Catholic, a rite that, like the Maronites, descends from the ancient Church of Antioch. Father McCarthy, known to the family as Father Charlie, is a man well acquainted with miracles and has formed very clear ideas about Audrey Santo's purpose and mission in this world.

Linda's mother was a Roman Catholic, and she and her husband attended Mass almost every day. When Linda reached her teens, she continued to be earnest about her religious life and even seriously thought about becoming a nun. She was attracted to the Carmelite order, which has a monastery just forty miles east of her home in the Roxbury section of Boston. At age fifteen Linda visited the monastery to talk to the nuns and become familiar with the contemplative, cloistered life the Carmelites lead.

For more than a hundred years, the Carmelites in Roxbury have lived in a monastery on Mount Pleasant Avenue. The Spanish architectural style of the redbrick building reflects the Spanish roots of the reformed Carmelite order. The day the nuns moved into the new building in 1897, more than two thousand people were given a tour through rooms that would never be open to the public again. They saw the chapter room on the second floor, which would be devoted to solemn religious exercises; peeked into the hermitage, a small alcove for isolated solitude; and looked into the individual cells where the nuns would sleep. A September 1897 *Boston Globe* article about the "open house" described the humble cells that were designed to reflect the simple and austere tradition of the order:

> It will surprise some readers to know that they are all furnished with gas light and steam heat. For the rest, each cell has a bed consisting of a rough box turned bottom side up, on which is laid a coarse mattress, and pillow, and a couple of dark blankets. There is a washstand with one drawer, and the toilet apparatus is of the poorest and plainest. This stand must serve also as a writing table at need. There is one rough wooden chair. Over the bed hangs a large cross—not a crucifix—of unpainted wood, fastened to the wall by large wooden nails. Three cheaply framed prints of Our Lady of Mount Carmel, St. Teresa and St. John of the Cross complete the furnishing of the cell.[11]

The rough box that served as the bed was actually a coffin placed upside down. After the nun's death, she would be buried in it. Other features of the monastery were black gratings that separated the nuns from visitors in the parlor rooms. A visitor could speak to the nun through the grating, and any objects brought into the monastery were passed through a set of revolving, barrel-shaped "turns." In the pretty, stained-glass-windowed chapel, which is open to the public, another grating isolated the nuns within their own section, called the choir. In keeping with Carmelite tradition, there are no pews in the choir because the nuns stand through all their devotions. Another important aspect of the Carmelite life is fasting and a very sparse vegetarian diet.

The gratings have been removed in recent years, but they were still intact when young Linda Nader visited in the 1960s. The lifestyle that Linda witnessed among these nuns was quiet, contemplative, and structured around regular devotions. The Discalced (barefoot or sandal-clad) Carmelite order was founded in the sixteenth century by Saint Teresa of Ávila (1515–82), who successfully separated from the original Carmelite order, which she felt had drifted from its pure and strict beginnings. The first Carmelites were an anonymous group of hermits who traveled to Mount Carmel, which lies on the northwest coast of what is now Israel, on the Mediterranean Sea, in the early 1200s. These men devoted themselves to a life of prayer based on the Old Testament prophet Elijah, who was historically very connected to the site. In the eighth century B.C., Elijah set up a challenge on Mount Carmel to test the power of the god Baal, who had been introduced by Queen Jezebel, and the God of Moses. Sacrifices were placed on two altars, and each side would pray to its divinity to ignite the fire. After several tries the priests of Baal gave up in disgust, but after just one prayer Elijah's altar burst into flames. Inspired by the prayerful and zealous life of Elijah, the thirteenth-century hermits sought to imitate his example on the mountainside of Carmel. Later, persecution against Christians forced the order to Europe, where it gradually followed a less rigorous tradition. Not until the sixteenth century would it be renewed by the efforts of a nun who became one of the most important Christian writers and mystics in the history of the Catholic Church.

Saint Teresa of Ávila has been an inspiration to Catholic girls for centuries, and Linda Santo was no exception. As Teresa's well-known story begins, she is a pious girl who enters the convent in her hometown at age eighteen. Teresa Sánchez de Cepeda y Ahumada eventually asked her superiors for permission to open a convent where she and a small group of nuns could return to the more solemn rules of the thirteenth-century Carmelite founders. She faced opposition from the order as well as from townspeople who didn't want to put up the finances to support another convent, but eventually her request was granted. Teresa's reforms became popular among both priests and nuns who wanted to return to a contemplative life of prayer. At the request of bishops in Spain and according to instructions she received during private spiritual revelations, Teresa traveled throughout the country setting up new convents. She had founded fifteen by the time she died in 1582, and in the next eighteen years the order grew to include thirty-two more convents of the Discalced Carmelites. The order continued to spread throughout Europe and the world, and today it is the best-known order of cloistered nuns.

Saint Teresa is recognized as one of the greatest mystics in the history of the Church and is admired for her combination of down-to-earth common sense and amazing supernatural experiences. She had conversations with Jesus and the saints, saw and understood the actions of evil spirits, discovered a technique of inner prayer, and was swept into ecstatic raptures that sometimes lifted her body off the ground. Her fellow nuns grew accustomed to being asked to hold Teresa down when she began levitating because she didn't want to draw attention to herself. Without adept spiritual mentors to guide her, she struggled alone through most of her experiences and learned to distinguish between divine information and temptations, between real prayer and intellectual distractions, and came to a deep understanding of other difficult issues on the religious path. She relied on the information she received in visions more than on the sporadic spiritual direction she received from her superiors and was able to clearly detail her progress in prayer and other devotions as a guide for others. "It is strange," she wrote, "what a difference there is between understanding a thing and subsequently knowing it by experience."[12] Saint Teresa's writings—especially *The Interior Castle* and her autobiography, *The Life of Saint Teresa of Ávila by Herself*—were very popular in her own time and have become classics of Christian literature. Saint Teresa Benedicta of the Cross (Edith Stein), the twentieth-century Carmelite nun who was declared a saint by Pope John Paul II in 1998, converted to Catholicism after reading Saint Teresa's autobiography.

The Carmelite nuns in Roxbury follow a routine that is focused on the inner life as expressed by Saint Teresa of Ávila. At least one hour is spent in personal prayer in the morning and in the evening, and one hour out of every day is devoted to spiritual reading. Five times during the day, the community gathers together to say the Liturgy of the Hours, a service of psalms, hymns, prayers, and biblical and spiritual readings. They also celebrate the Eucharist every day in a Mass spoken by one of the parish priests. For much of the day the nuns pray and work in silence, reserving conversation for meals and specific times of recreation. About four hours of the day are given to manual labor performed in silence, such as cooking, gardening, sewing, sweeping, and other household tasks. By living this way, the nuns at the Carmelite monastery

> witness to the contemplative dimension in every person, to that inner urging to find meaning in something, Someone beyond the self, seeking the fulfillment of the deepest aspirations within each heart for what is true, noble and best. Thus we serve our brothers and sisters everywhere, that all of us together may find the center where we may be one as Jesus is one with the Father. In the Teresian Carmel, each person is called to be our Lord's good friend, totally surrendered to His love and transformed by the process of prayer into a living flame of love for God and for His people.[13]

The usual requirements for admission to the Carmelite order are physical, mental, and emotional health; a high-school education; and some college or equivalent work experience. After initial interviews, some monasteries allow the potential candidate to live in the convent/monastery for six weeks to experience the day-to-day life before making a formal application. If the person agrees to stay, the candidacy period lasts from six months to a year and is followed by a novitiate of one to two years. A three-year commitment is then followed by final vows, in which the woman or man officially becomes a Carmelite.

Silence, prayer, reading, chores performed in solitude, hours in the chapel: this was the contemplative life that Linda explored when she visited the nuns in Roxbury. The rooms and furnishings were much the same as they had been when the nuns first moved into the building in 1897, including the beds made of rough mattresses filled with straw. Although Carmelite policy does not allow anyone under the age of eighteen to enter the order, the nuns allowed overnight visits for girls like Linda who were exploring the Carmelite way of life. Linda met with at least one issue in convent life that she couldn't bear—the straw in the mattresses upset her allergies. After her short visit with the sisters on Mount Pleasant Avenue, she gave up her desire to become a nun.

In spite of her change of heart over the religious life, Linda Santo has said that she's always been a "Jesus freak." Energetic, sprightly and a petite four-eleven, Linda has the no-nonsense look of a busy mom and tries to take the onslaught of public attention in stride. She is continually surprised with visitors showing up from faraway states or countries and will sometimes relieve the volunteer and stop to tell the visitors Audrey's story herself. Counting off the miracles and explaining the role of victim soul, which she believes has been divinely conferred upon Audrey, Linda speaks with conviction.

Linda Santo has always drawn strength from her faith, especially as a mother. She faced tough challenges with the birth of each of her four children, who all struggled with serious medical problems in infancy. Matthew and Jennifer, Linda's two eldest children from her first marriage, which ended in divorce, were both born with heart problems.

Matthew was in and out of the hospital with repeated episodes of cardiac arrest. Jennifer's heart problems required open-heart surgery, and she was bedridden until she was six years old.[14] Stephen and Audrey, the children of Linda's second marriage, to Stephen Santo, were also born with heart problems. Stephen, who is one year older than Audrey, suffered from a coarctation (narrowing) of the aorta, a condition that raises the blood pressure in the upper body and lowers the blood pressure in the legs and trunk. Audrey was born with atrial septal defect, a hole in the wall between the top two chambers of the heart. This condition puts a higher demand on the heart and causes more blood to go to the lungs—leading to respiratory problems. In addition to her heart defect, Audrey suffered from apnea, which caused her breathing to stop at times. These apnea spells decrease the heart rate, decreasing the blood flow and the amount of oxygen in the bloodstream.

Audrey was a premature baby, born eight weeks early. She was not, however, the only special-needs patient when she was born two months early on December 19, 1983. In the video entitled *The Story of Little Audrey Santo* (produced, written, and directed by a member of the volunteer organization dedicated to Audrey), viewers learn that Linda was very ill when she was pregnant with Audrey. In this film Linda's sister, Jeri Cox, says, "My sister had cancer and was not able to conceive, and Audrey was conceived."[15] Author Thomas Petrisko wrote that Linda had cervical, uterine, and breast cancer when Audrey was born, adding that the infant Audrey "somehow seemed to be related to a miraculous healing of her own mother. Not long afterward, Linda's cancer was . . . diagnosed as having mysteriously vanished."[16] The *20/20* feature on Audrey Santo states that Linda was diagnosed with breast cancer years after Audrey's accident and that she cut her chemotherapy program short so she would have more time and energy to devote to Audrey.

The special needs of a child like Audrey would be taxing for any couple. They would be extremely demanding on a single parent, which is what Linda became shortly after Audrey's drowning accident. When Linda and her children brought Audrey home from the hospital four months later, they came home without a father. Linda, then age thirty-nine, and Stephen, age twenty-four, had been married for six years, but while Audrey was in the hospital, he left the family. "I'm not afraid to tell people about this part of my life," he told the *Worcester Telegram & Gazette* in January 2000. "I was born an alcoholic and then I really started to drink after the accident happened. I thought that I had been dealt a bad roll of the dice. My life was a mess and I really went to the dogs. I could only cope with the help of the bottle."[17] Stephen, a handsome, strapping man with a blue-collar Boston-area accent, told the reporter that he blamed himself for being at work instead of at home on the Sunday morning when Audrey fell into the pool. He also felt guilty about building a bigger pool in the backyard instead of just keeping the smaller one that came with the house.

Steve's alcohol and drug problems escalated over the next months and years until everything came to a crashing halt one winter night in 1991. On January 31 he stole a car that was parked outside a store in Worcester. The driver had gone into the store, leaving a four-year-old child inside the car.

Steve Santo took the child out of the vehicle, left him standing on the curb, and drove off. A few hours later he robbed
a gas station at gunpoint in the nearby town of Clinton. The
stolen car had been reported by then, and a few minutes after he left the gas station, he was spotted by the police, who
tried to pull him over. Steve led the police on a chase and
tried to ram into two of the police cruisers. On the second try
he hit a meridian, rolled his car, got out, and tried to run away
from the police. They quickly caught up to him, however,
and Steve was arrested. He pleaded guilty to armed robbery,
threat to commit murder, assault and battery by means of
a dangerous weapon, larceny, and other offenses. He was
sentenced to eight-to-twelve years at the state's maximum-
security prison, where his counselors diagnosed him with a
serious and long-standing alcohol and drug addiction.

In the meantime, Linda had a disabled child to care for
and three other children to raise. She had seen Steve's drug
and alcohol problems lead to trouble before, and the de-
mands on her time prevented her from worrying about him
or wondering about their future together. "I was just too
damned busy to think about his leaving," she said. "I think
he really had to hit bottom to turn his life around."[18]

During the next few years in prison, Stephen got drug-
and alcohol-rehabilitation counseling and took several
courses to turn his life around, such as Anger Management
and Alternatives to Violence. Linda wrote to the court to explain that Steve's problems arose from a dependency that
"has proven on many occasions to act for him" and to request that Steve's sentence be shortened because "a program
with direction and guidance to free him from his problems is

a far better solution than bonding him with criminals in a state prison."[19] Steve was released from prison in January 1996, after serving five years. He and Linda renewed their wedding vows that year, and Steve moved home to South Flagg Street. Looking back, Steve realizes that his night of crime in 1991 was a wake-up call that probably saved his life. "In a strange way, it's a good thing that I got arrested," he said. "I could still be out there drinking, or, even worse, dead. Now I get up in the morning and I can remember what I did the night before."[20] Linda and Steve attribute their reconciliation to Audrey, calling it "one of Audrey's biggest miracles." To them, the healing and forgiveness that brought them together again were gifts that flowed from her.

⁕ ⁕ ⁕

When Linda brought Audrey home from the hospital in late 1987, the family began a new life in a house bustling with the commotion of dozens of people coming and going every day: nurses, physical therapists, doctors, and friends and relatives who wanted to help out. In the midst of all the activity, Linda Santo began making plans to give Audrey the chance for a miracle. She had read about the apparitions of the Virgin Mary at Medjugorje in what was then Yugoslavia and the miracles that thousands of people had claimed from visits there. Since June 24, 1981 (the same day, the family points out, that Linda and Stephen were married), Mary has reportedly appeared to a group of six young people in this village nestled in a region that has been the site of one of the bloodiest wars in modern history. Linda sent a letter and a picture of Audrey to Maria Pavolvic, one of the visionaries, in early 1988. She then learned that Maria gave the picture to the Virgin Mary during a vision and that Mary embraced Audrey. Linda also learned that when Mary is asked to intercede for sick children, she often gives the visionary special instructions to bring back to the parents, such as directions to fast or pray. Instead of these instructions, the Blessed Virgin simply embraced Audrey in the apparition. Linda wrote more letters and continued to call the administrative office of the Medjugorje shrine as she pieced together a plan that many thought was ridiculous. Inspired by the miraculous stories surrounding the visionaries, she decided to take Audrey to Medjugorje in faraway, unstable Yugoslavia. Linda realizes that some of the decisions she's made may appear crazy, but she's not concerned with what people think. "I know I seem insane," she told the *Washington Post* in the summer of 1998. "I'm in good company. Half the saints were insane."[21] She would need all the self-confidence and fortitude she could muster in the harrowing trip that was to follow.

Eventually, Linda received an invitation to bring Audrey to the apparition room at the St. James Church in Medjugorje. That room had been closed to the public for a year, but a rare exception was granted in this case—bolstering Linda's belief that something special would happen on the trip. One of the women from St. James warned Linda that the choir loft, where the apparitions take place, could be entered only by climbing a steep and winding stairway. Taking a disabled child and her medical equipment up those steps would be difficult, if not impossible. Linda said that she would carry Audrey up there on her knees if she had to.

The Santos visited Medjugorje in 1988, before the breakup of communist Yugoslavia and the war that lasted from 1991 to 1995. Medjugorje lies on the western edge of Bosnia-Herzegovina, about twenty miles inland from the Adriatic Sea. In a straight line across the sea lies the town of Vieste, on the east coast of Italy. Since the apparitions began in 1981, more than 20 million people have traveled to Medjugorje. The visits slowed down during the war in Bosnia but didn't stop entirely. This small village was not touched by violence throughout the war, even though it lies just a few miles west of Mostar, where 2,000 people were killed, 26,000 left as refugees, and 5,000 buildings were destroyed.

The Medjugorje apparitions began on a June evening in 1981, when six children (five of them adolescents) saw a beautiful young woman with a baby in her arms on the hillside. She gestured for them to come closer, but even though they each had a strong feeling that she was Mary, they were too frightened to go near her and ran home. The next day, June 25, four of the children plus two others returned to the same place on the hillside with a little more courage and hopes of seeing the lady again. After a sudden flash of light, she appeared once again, smiling and happy, this time without the baby. Her appearances continued, and by the fifth day a crowd of fifteen thousand had gathered on the hill to be in the presence of the apparition. The lady identified herself as the Blessed Virgin Mary and would appear to this same group every day for many years. She continues to appear to some of them daily (wherever they are) and others just once a month or once a year. One of the visionaries, Ivan Dragicevic, described his visionary experience to an audience in Seattle in October 1997, immediately after receiving his daily apparition:

> A light comes and then after the light, she comes. When our Lady came tonight she was joyous. She greeted us all at the beginning, "Praise be Jesus! My Dear Children!" Then our Lady prayed over all of us with extended hands. She blessed us all. . . . I see our Lady just like I see you and I speak to her freely like I speak to you. I am telling you the truth when I say that I am much more relaxed speaking to her than to you. I can also touch our Lady. . . . She has a gray dress, white veil, blue eyes, and rosy cheeks and black hair. She stands on a cloud and has a crown of stars above her head.[22]

For the past eighteen years the messages given to the Medjugorje visionaries and shared with the world have stressed five themes: peace, faith, conversion, prayer, and fasting.

The apparitions at Medjugorje have not yet been officially sanctioned by the Catholic Church as have those at Fátima, Lourdes, and elsewhere. It usually takes many years for places of pilgrimage to be recognized by the Church, with the exception of Lourdes, which was approved only four years after the apparitions began. Even though Medjugorje is not a fully approved pilgrimage site, the Church does not prohibit visits by the faithful, even priests. Priests or other clergy are not allowed, however, to organize and lead official pilgrimages. Pope John Paul II appears to be supportive of Medjugorje, and there is a strong consensus that the site will one day be approved by the Vatican.

Like millions of pilgrims before her, Linda Santo planned a visit to the shrine in the hope that a healing would take place. People are drawn to Medjugorje, Fátima, Lourdes, Guadalupe, and La Salette to be in the presence of Mary, whom they believe visits these places, even if they don't see her themselves. Thousands of apparitions of Mary have occurred throughout Church history, but their number increased dramatically in the nineteenth and twentieth centuries. In the United States twenty-nine apparition sites have sprung up since World War II in locations including Scottsdale, Arizona; Cincinnati, Ohio; Detroit, Michigan; Denver, Colorado; Bayside and Brooklyn, New York; and Conyers, Georgia. None of the Marian apparitions in the United States have been formally approved by the Catholic Church, however.

The presence of Mary in Medjugorje, whether officially recognized by the Church or not, was irresistible to Linda Santo; she felt that Audrey might have a chance of healing in such a holy place. Linda's faith was supported by a centuries-old tradition of belief in Mary's presence in the world. Mary's appearance all over the globe in modern times continues the legendary history of veneration of the Holy Mother. In the Middle Ages Mary was an extremely important figure in the minds of Catholics in Europe, especially France, where her veneration was expressed in the Gothic cathedral. Notre Dame (Our Lady) of Chartres, Reims, Paris—each of these magnificent buildings was dedicated to the feminine member of the divine family. In medieval Europe people were drawn to Mary as a protectress and as someone to whom they could relate more easily than to

Christ and God the Father, who loomed as judgmental figures. Colorful legends sprang up around the Holy Mother, who put corrupt clergymen in their place and granted special favors to the knights in her service. Jesus was more approachable through his mother, and the mother-son relationship was celebrated in cathedral architecture. In *Mont Saint Michel and Chartres* (1904), Henry Adams describes the medieval desire for the divine Mother who was more accessible and understanding than the all-perfect Father, Son, and Holy Ghost: "The Mother alone was human, imperfect, and could love. . . . The Mother alone could represent whatever was not Unity; whatever was irregular, exceptional, outlawed; and this was the whole human race."[23] Through the intercession of Mary, people from every part of society felt they had a better chance of receiving God's mercy. This relationship with Mary was the driving force behind the extravagant amount of time and money given to building cathedrals dedicated to her:

> Just as the French in the nineteenth century invested their surplus capital in a railway-system in the belief that they would make money by it in this life, in the thirteenth they trusted their money to the Queen of Heaven because of their belief in her power to repay it with interest in the life to come. The investment was based on the power of Mary as Queen rather than on any orthodox church-conception. . . . Had the Church controlled her, the Virgin would perhaps have remained prostrate at the foot of the Cross.[24]

"Nearly every great church of the twelfth and thirteenth centuries belongs to Mary," wrote Adams. "If you are to get the full enjoyment of Chartes, you must . . . feel her presence as the architects did, in every stone they placed, and every touch they chiseled."[25] Many people also experience this unearthly "presence" when visiting apparition sites. You don't have to be Catholic to taste this presence; people of all faiths have had profound experiences on the hilltop at Medjugorje, in front of the grotto in Lourdes—and in the Santo family's home chapel. The accounts of Mary's presence at apparition sites, in cathedrals, and elsewhere share a common thread of distinct feeling. I was raised as a Protestant in a church that gave little attention to Mary. One of the few times Jesus' mother was mentioned in a service was on Christmas Eve, when Sunday-school children dressed up in robes to portray Joseph and Mary in the live manger scene at the front of the church. Otherwise, Mary was rarely mentioned throughout the liturgical year. In spite of this, I have strongly sensed her presence in various places. In Lourdes, where I was doing research for a previous book, the atmosphere was filled with an almost palpable sense of peace and unconditional love. This unique sense of presence had come to me before, in Chartres. Just before I left my hotel room to walk to the cathedral on the edge of town, I felt a surge of this feeling; when I entered the cathedral itself, I was immersed in it to the point of tears. Among the few other places in which I have felt this unique presence is the Santo chapel. The sheen of oil that covered practically every item in the place did not move me nearly as much as the distinct feeling of Mary's presence in that small room.

It's difficult to describe how Mary is so clearly identified with this feeling. In the rare instances when I've felt her presence, why haven't I interpreted it as that of Jesus, the Holy Spirit, or a guardian angel? There was simply no question that it was Mary, and this is the same explanation given by many people who have written about their personal encounters with her. In *The Religious Function of the Psyche,* Jungian analyst Lionel Corbett, M.D., writes about an encounter with Mary's presence that he experienced during a session with a client. The patient, a man being treated for chronic depression, told Dr. Corbett about something that happened in his childhood after a traumatic event. His mother died in a fire in the basement, and he hadn't heard anything because he was playing in a remote part of the house. His father blamed him for not helping his mother, and the guilt—coupled with the shock of losing his mother—crushed him. That night a radiant vision of the Virgin Mary appeared at the foot of the boy's bed and consoled him deeply. He had been able to recall this vision and derive comfort from it for the rest of his life. Mary's presence manifested itself during the telling of this childhood memory in Dr. Corbett's office. "Even though this experience had occurred many years before," wrote Dr. Corbett, "characteristically its numinosity [divine nature] affected us both as soon as the story was told, and the presence of the Mother archetype was palpable in the room."[26] Welcoming this presence, accepting it as something real, became a vital part of the man's therapy thereafter.

Corbett's approach to the religious aspect of our lives focuses on our personal experience with the divine, an experience that is completely independent of religious doctrine. "The religious approach to the psyche is thus directly in accord with the mystical traditions of all world religions, in that it tries to approach the divine (or transcendent levels of reality) by locating it directly and deeply within ourselves." His book describes numinous experiences as natural events that spring from the human psyche (the conscious and unconscious mind). We usually filter these divine experiences through familiar images: in the example above, the boy viewed the divine presence as Mary. But according to Corbett's method, that is just one identity given to a universal archetype, or inborn pattern, that affects all of us. The apparitions of Mary that are so prevalent in the world today are manifestations of a basic archetype, the Mother, as well as of the goddess and the feminine aspect of the divine. In a materialist, high-tech, scientific, environment-bashing world ridden with wars and nuclear armament, it's not difficult to consider the theory that divinity is trying to speak through compassionate, loving mother images. Traditionally, apparitions of Mary have occurred in areas hit by war, poverty, or other great strife.

By appearing all over the world, the visions of Mary may be creating balance in the unspiritual, "unnatural," technology-dependent atmosphere of modern life. Because they are mysterious and hark back to an age when the supernatural was embraced rather than scorned, these visions open a safety valve to this neglected aspect of life. "The increase in reports of apparitions," wrote Reverend Johann Roten, "may suggest that there is a spiritual hunger today that goes beyond institutional churches." Reverend Roten, a priest who directs the Marian Research Institute at the University of Dayton, added, "There's a need for the mystery to be put back in people's lives. Apparitions may be one of God's many answers to these needs."[27]

The image of Mary—in pictures and statues rather than as apparitions—would come to play a large part in the Santo family home as the focus of extraordinary miracles. News of these phenomena would spread to the faithful who, for many reasons, sought out the presence of Mary. Whether through verbal messages like those given the visionaries at Fátima or physical signs like those surrounding Audrey Santo, many believe that Mary is speaking to the world.

Monsignor Vincent Keane, a priest at Our Lady of the Blessed Sacrament in Queens, New York, believes that Marian apparitions spread the message that we should try to trust more in God than shoulder all of our responsibilities alone. He sees Mary's life as a lesson in trust, a lesson that we can all learn by listening to her. "The number of appearances of the Blessed Mother seems to be abounding these days," he said, "so there must be some reason for it. The only thing that I can think of is that, with regard to the role of the Blessed Mother, she has a very specific role in the history of salvation for Christians. As the angel Gabriel appeared to her and said she would be the mother of this child, the son of God, her great concern was: How can this be? If I haven't had any relations, how can this be? The whole concern of Mary was that she wanted to do right and she didn't understand. But the angel Gabriel told her that she had to trust that the work of God would be accomplished. When she's appearing in the world, the message to people is always: Do not be afraid, you've got to trust. Now, sometimes the message is also about sin; sin has to be avoided, there has to be penance, and you have to perform certain actions—but the message is always the message of a loving mother. I think of ourselves completing one millennium and heading into another, and there are endless hopes of what we'd like to see. We'd like to see peace, and we look at all the difficulties in the world and wonder if there can ever be peace. And God is telling us there can be. It seems to me the Blessed Mother continually promises as a mother to tell us: Do not be afraid. Nothing is impossible, Mary is here. Mary is the mother and she takes care.

"The very final words of Christ in John's gospel," Father Keane continued, "when he's hanging on the cross and he sees his mother and John, is a dramatic moment. He says to Mary, 'Woman, behold your son,' and to John, for all of us, 'Behold your mother.' Dramatically, at the end of his life, he gives us Mary as our mother. Not only is she his mother, she's our mother forever. If you think of it, with all the trouble in the world, it seems God in his goodness is sending us this person who we should not be afraid of at all. She will do anything for us. The message is: No matter what the difficulties and trials, she is the one who is taking care of us."

In *Blessed Among Women: Encounters with Mary and Her Message,* G. Scott Sparrow describes Mary's appearance in the modern world as a call to develop our nurturing nature and undertake the difficult path of "becoming 'mothers' of all creation by awakening to a timeless, moment-to-moment appreciation for one another and all creatures." In this spirit, we can infuse Mary's motherly love into everything we do. Sparrow believes that Mary's inspiration is available to those of all faiths and cultures:

> In whatever form we can know her best, and through whatever spiritual tradition answers to our needs, the Holy Mother wants us to do a great work together— to become like her and to offer up what God requests of us without quibbling over the fine points of religious beliefs. . . . It all comes down to one question: *Will you do what the Spirit asks of you?*[28]

. . .

Many miracles have been attributed to the Marian shrines throughout the world, including Medjugorje. Linda Santo, whose sister had given her reading material about the shrine after Audrey came home from the hospital, believed that it was a powerful place of healing and was determined to take Audrey there. One of the most widely published miracle stories about Medjugorje took place during the first week that the apparitions began in 1981. Mr. and Mrs. Setka brought their two-and-a-half-year-old son, Daniel, to Medjugorje on June 28, the fifth day of Mary's appearances. Just after his birth, Daniel had contracted septicemia—blood poisoning— which threw him into convulsions and left him unable to speak. His head was permanently tilted to the right, and he couldn't take more than a step or two without falling. Mr. Setka asked the visionaries to intercede with the Holy Mother for his son, but they were overwhelmed with requests that day and asked the family to return the next day. They came back to the hillside on June 29, and after the apparition, visionary Jakov Colo told them that Mary spoke to him about Daniel. She told him that if the parents were to believe firmly, the boy would be healed. On the way home the family stopped at a restaurant, where, to everyone's amazement, Daniel said, "Give me something to drink." From that moment on he began putting words together and speaking like a normal toddler, and his walking improved to the point that he was soon climbing stairs and kicking a soccer ball around the yard. Inspired by these and many other miraculous healings that occurred from the very start of the apparitions, Linda Santo hoped that Audrey's miracle was waiting for her in Medjugorje. She packed Audrey's sandals for the trip, hoping that her little girl would be able to run down Apparition Hill.

Audrey's pediatricians, Dr. John Riordon and Dr. Edward Kaye, gave Linda permission to take her daughter on this long journey. One of Linda's close friends, registered nurse Joyce O'Neill, agreed to join them to help with Audrey's medical care, and the three of them left for Bosnia-Herzegovina on July 29, 1988. They took an ambulance from Worcester to New York's John F. Kennedy Airport, where they had made reservations for six seats on a Yugoslav Airlines flight to Dubrovnik. Audrey's stretcher would be placed across a row of three seats. These special arrangements had been planned in advance, and Linda was relieved that the airline was so accommodating. "They've really been good and have been most cooperative," she said just before the trip.[29]

Landing at Dubrovnik gave Linda and Joyce a quick reality check on the nation they would be visiting for the next two weeks. Machine-gun-toting guards patrolled the airport, and the ambulance they had ordered turned out to be a very old model that didn't have a rear door. With Audrey lying on a stretcher in the heat, surrounded by a horde of medical equipment and luggage, Linda and Joyce negotiated with the officials for the use of an old government van that had sliding doors to accommodate the stretcher and equipment. Once everything was in place, the three Americans and their driver headed up the coast for the three-hour drive to Medjugorje.

Arrangements had been made for Linda, Joyce, and Audrey to stay with a local family in the village. As they made their way into the house with tiny Audrey on the stretcher, her respirator and other equipment trailing behind, dozens of English-speaking pilgrims gathered around and introduced themselves. Inside the house they were greeted by their host Croatian family, one of whom also spoke English. Linda and Joyce got Audrey settled in their rented room upstairs and, exhausted from the long trip, looked forward to a good night's sleep. There was more in store for them on that first night, however. Sitting at Audrey's bedside, Linda heard a commotion in the street below. The voices got louder, and she heard people yelling that the little American girl's face was "in the moon." Linda ran to the window and saw a sea of hands pointing up to the sky. She looked up at the moon and saw her daughter's face, complete with the wavy outline of her hair against her cheek. This miraculous event caused a stir the next day, and Linda and Joyce met people from all over the world. That night the miracle repeated itself. This time Linda and the crowd saw two moons in the sky: one with the face of Audrey, and one with the face of a woman Linda described as "an old nun."[30]

These inexplicable visions, seen by many people, filled Linda with an even deeper expectation that Audrey would be healed there. She was scheduled to bring Audrey to the apparition room on the third evening of their stay. That day they gave themselves plenty of time to get Audrey into a taxi, drive to St. James Church, make their way through the throng of thousands surrounding the building, and climb up to the choir room in time for the 6:40 apparition. Everything went smoothly, and suddenly Linda and Joyce found themselves sitting in a sparse, stiflingly hot choir loft with Ivan Dragicevic, one of the visionaries. Audrey lay on her stretcher directly below the spot where the Lady is said to hover before the visionaries. Even though the air was perfectly still, with no windows open or fans blowing, Audrey's hair moved slightly as if a soft breeze were flowing over her during the apparition. After about seven minutes, Ivan came out of his ecstatic trance and walked over to Audrey. He knelt next to her and spoke to her in Croatian for a few minutes. Then they were all dismissed, and the group made their way down the winding steps. Outside, Linda and Joyce were snapped out of their awestruck mood when the crowd suddenly started crushing them in an attempt to touch the little girl who had just been in the presence of the apparition. They shouldered their way through to the waiting taxi and breathed a sigh of relief when they were safely inside.

While the apparition was taking place, Linda had prayed to the Virgin Mary, asking her to either heal Audrey or take her. Her daughter wasn't healed, but up in the choir loft she seemed to have been affected by something. Linda recalled that everyone was sweating profusely from the heat, but Audrey did not have a drop on her face. Linda had wiped the sweat from her daughter on the long drive from Dubrovnik, so she knew that Audrey could perspire normally. Also, during the apparition Linda had a strong sense that Audrey and the Virgin Mary were communicating with each other. Even though Audrey didn't get up from her stretcher and walk into her arms, Linda felt that something happened in that room that night. For the next three days she spent hours praying by Audrey's side. To take a break, she walked through the village, talked to pilgrims, and looked forward to the next visit with the visionary.

On the evening of her second appointment, Audrey was once again brought up to the choir loft to be in the room when Ivan received the apparition. Just as he had done the first time, Ivan knelt next to Audrey after the vision was over and spoke to her in Croatian. Linda never learned what Ivan said to Audrey. "I never found out and I never asked him," she said. "I figured if I were supposed to know, he'd tell me."[31]

Audrey didn't wake up from her semicomatose state during the second apparition, but something dramatic did happen later that night. After the apparition Linda and Joyce took Audrey back down the stairs, fought the crowd to get to the taxi, and went home. Less than two hours later, Audrey suddenly began to move. Her legs and arms came to life and her eyes focused on Joyce and appeared to be sensitive to light. Linda and Joyce let out screams of joy, and the Croatian family ran up to the room. Everyone was hugging and crying and laughing until Audrey stopped—completely. She fell back on the bed. "Then she died," said Linda.

Even though Linda had prayed for Audrey to be either healed or taken by God, her maternal instincts took over when Audrey's heart stopped beating. She and Joyce immediately began CPR, and a few minutes later they got a pulse. They borrowed a car and rushed Audrey to the nearest hospital, about thirty minutes away. This small clinic didn't have any oxygen, which Audrey desperately needed to assist her breathing, so they drove on to the city of Zagreb. After a three-hour drive north through the mountains, they were refused admission to the hospital. They turned back and drove south to Mostar, the city just twenty miles east of Medjugorje. Throughout this wild, nightmarish night of driving from hospital to hospital, Audrey's heart stopped five times. She didn't stabilize until she was settled in the Mostar hospital. The medical facility there was primitive at best, and Linda knew she had to get Audrey back to the United States as soon as possible. Two years later Linda would learn that not only were abortions performed in the Mostar hospital, it served as the largest abortion clinic in Yugoslavia. She believes that everything that happens in Audrey's life carries a special meaning, and the proximity of Medjugorje to the abortion clinic in Mostar is no exception. Linda has stated that Audrey's survival in Bosnia-Herzegovina symbolizes that she is a testament to life in a world that condones abortion.

Yugoslav Airlines would not take Audrey home in her condition, so Linda called her niece back home and asked her to track down a medical plane. Cynthia Norton, Audrey's cousin, frantically tried to find a private medical-transport company that could leave immediately. She was in for a big disappointment. "They said it would cost from $40,000 to $60,000," she told the *Worcester Telegram & Gazette*, "and the majority of them couldn't come until [the] next week. The longer Audrey was there, the worse her condition got."[32] With private airlines ruled out, Cynthia turned to the government for help. She called the office of her U.S. Congressman, Joseph D. Early of Worcester, whose aides quickly got in touch with the State Department in Washington. A medically equipped air force plane was put on reserve to pick up Audrey, Linda, and Joyce the next day. The flight wasn't free, however. The plane could not leave the ground before the family paid a $25,000 fee. Audrey's grandmother, Pat Nader, set up a quick meeting with the bank and remortgaged a property (a house she owned in addition to the one on South Flagg Street). The money was wired to Washington, and the plane took off on Friday, August 6. With one stop in Germany to switch planes, the group flew back in a state-of-the-art military plane to Washington, then took a private medical plane to the Worcester airport. Audrey was immediately taken to St. Vincent's Hospital in an ambulance with a police escort.

The day they arrived home, Cynthia Norton was asked by a reporter whether Linda Santo was disillusioned by the near tragic turn of her trip in search for a miracle. "She's a very religious woman of strong faith," Cynthia said. "She feels that whatever happens is meant to be."[33]

• • •

Audrey's encounter with Mary in Medjugorje did not produce a miracle. Four weeks after she arrived home, however, a miraculous event in the Santo home seemed to herald that Mary was with them.

In September 1988 David Ethier of Rhode Island came to Worcester with a statue of Mary in the likeness of her appearances at Fátima, Portugal. During the week, David worked with computers, but on the weekends he traveled all over New England with the plaster "pilgrim statue" to which physical and spiritual healings and other miracles had been attributed. According to David, the tradition of placing one of these statues in a different home from week to week began in Fátima in the 1940s and has since spread throughout the world. His wife bought the statue for him and had it blessed by a priest. Four years earlier David received permission from the Worcester diocese to bring his statue into the community. "When she goes into a home," he said, "their faith is blessed. I believe in spiritual healings more than physical healings."[34]

The image of Our Lady of Fátima is a reminder of a miracle that has been described as the greatest supernatural occurrence of the twentieth century. This miracle, witnessed by tens of thousands of people in 1917, occurred during an apparition of Mary. The Fátima apparitions began on May 13 of that year, when three children out in the hills tending sheep saw two bright flashes of light in the sky. They wondered how there could be lightning when there were no clouds. As they moved the herd, they suddenly saw a lady, surrounded by light, hovering above a tree. She asked them to return to the site on the same day, at the same time, for the next six months. In the course of their visions, the three children received many messages for the world as well as a three-part secret. The first two parts were made public, and the third part of the message was sealed and stored away in the Vatican until June 2000. The primary messages Mary gave to Lucia, Jacinta, and Francisco dealt with the world's need to pray the rosary and to do penance so that people would be converted. Her messages included predictions and warnings of events that could occur if the world did not turn to God.

Mary told the children, "On the last month, I will perform a miracle so that all may believe." By this time tens of thousands of people were flocking to Fátima on the thirteenth of each month to watch the visionaries, the strange colors in the sky, and the mysterious events that surrounded the apparitions. On October 13 an event took place that has come to be known as the Miracle of the Sun. Exactly at the time the visionaries said it would happen, in the presence of seventy thousand eyewitnesses, the sun turned a silvery color and took the shape of a flat disc. Everyone could look at it without hurting their eyes. It spun rapidly and shot out streams of colored light in all directions. The spinning disc bounced, shook, and moved horizontally in the sky—then plunged toward the earth in a zigzag motion, growing larger as it got closer. The crowd began screaming in fear that it would crash upon them. But before it reached the earth, the disc suddenly shot back up with the same zigzag movement.

It then transformed into its normal shape, color, and blinding brilliance.

The Fátima apparitions were declared "worthy of belief" by the Catholic Church in 1930. Pope John Paul II credits Our Lady of Fátima for saving his life during the assassination attempt in St. Peter's Square in 1981.

The statue of Our Lady of Fátima was brought to the Santo home during the second week of September 1988. One of the supernatural phenomena associated with it, Mr. Ethier informed the families he visited, was its ability to change facial expressions. Mary's face would move as if it were alive. "The statue's expressions do change," he said. David brought the statue into Linda's house for a Saturday-night prayer service. Audrey was in her bed, in stable condition after her death-defying ordeal in Medjugorje. Linda and a group of friends and relatives were in the living room with the statue, getting ready for the prayer service. Our Lady of Fátima was placed on one side of the room in full view of each visitor. Suddenly, in front of everyone's eyes, it happened. The edges of the statue's mouth turned upward. "When she came in she was sad," said Linda. "Then she smiled." The statue renewed Linda's conviction that something special had happened at Medjugorje, something that would affect their lives forever.

With a room full of witnesses, Linda declared, "We've already had our first miracle."[35]

3.

Stigmata: The Sacred Wounds

*All of a sudden a great light shone round about
my eyes. In the midst of this light there appeared
the wounded Christ . . . all blood, from whom
there came forth beams of light with shafts of
flame that wounded me in the hands and feet.*
—Padre Pio[1]

*Audrey has suffered the Passion many, many
times. . . . During Lent, Audrey is in so much
pain.* —Linda Santo[2]

As hundreds stood in line in the Christ the King parking lot
on August 9, 1999, heat poured down from the cloudless
sky and rose up from the sweltering asphalt below. Marking
the twelfth anniversary of Audrey Santo's accident, this was
Anniversary Day, an annual event in Worcester in which Audrey is brought out in public for the benefit of those who
wish to see her. The line snaked through the lot, doubling
back on itself several times to hold as many visitors as possible. Some with more foresight than I brought folding chairs
and umbrellas, and many carried bottles of water. Tour buses
slowly made their way down Pleasant Street, stopping long
enough near the church to let passengers disembark.

The crowd was a mix of all ages, from families with infants

to teenagers to retired couples. In one section of the line a dozen parishioners from Brooklyn chatted in Italian as their priest made arrangements for the group to make a special private visit with Audrey. A TV journalist with a microphone walked up and down the line, shadowed by her cameraman, asking visitors where they came from and why. The woman in front of me shared her copy of the latest Audrey Santo newsletter with the people ahead of her and gave them a brief summary of Audrey's story, including an update on the hours that the chapel is open to the public. At the sidewalk, where the line made its final stretch before reaching the church doors, a sign informed us that

LITTLE AUDREY WILL BE IN THE CHURCH— YOU WILL SEE HER.

Those who stood nearest the church entrance watched as the police, emergency medical personnel, and priests hovered around the ambulance that had transported Audrey from her home a few blocks away. The ambulance was now parked on the sidewalk with its rear doors facing the entry to the church. At eleven o'clock the church doors opened and visitors slowly began filing by a team of ushers who handed out a flyer containing instructions for viewing Audrey: pause only briefly in front of Audrey, then move up to the front of the church.

More visitors continued to arrive as the earliest pilgrims slowly disappeared into the church. It took approximately an hour and a half for those who had been waiting near the center of the line to reach the doors. Two large baskets in the foyer invited visitors to drop off prayer requests. Once through the inner doors, the line moved along the wall to the left. About three feet away visitors passed the large glass window to the "crying room," where mothers bring their fidgeting babies during Mass so as not to disrupt the other worshipers. This day the crying room held Audrey Santo, lying on a gurney, covered from feet to chin with a white blanket. Her face was turned toward the window and her eyes were open. Linda Santo and a nurse stood behind the gurney, engaged in a conversation that no one could hear through the soundproof wall and glass.

Keeping the line slowly moving, we had only a few seconds to peer at Audrey as we passed by the window. For many, the long trip to Worcester and the long wait outside the church created a high level of anticipation that culminated in this brief glance. I couldn't brush aside the disturbing sense that I was gawking at a severely disabled child, her body seemingly invisible beneath the flat white blanket. Adding to this self-consciousness was the fact that a television camera was filming the entire experience. Standing on the back pew of the church, approximately five feet from the window, a cameraman focused his lens on the pilgrims as they filed past Audrey. Not only were we aware that we were staring, we knew that we were being watched and recorded as we did so.

Once the visitors moved beyond the window, they followed the line to the front of the church, where they could pause to kneel at the rail and pray before leaving through the side door. A young man sat at a portable electric piano in front of the lectern, playing a contemporary song about Audrey that rang quietly through the sanctuary. A few people chose to move out of line and into a pew to spend a few minutes in reflection, some praying silently with their rosary beads. Behind them the line continued to file in and pass by the glass window. By the end of the afternoon, approximately five thousand people had made the route through the church.

The year before, Audrey's anniversary day was celebrated in a much larger venue: the 23,500-seat Fitton Field football stadium in Worcester. On the campus of Holy Cross, a Jesuit college, this outdoor stadium is near Interstate 290, which leads into downtown Worcester. The heat was in full force on August 9, 1998, too, when approximately eight thousand people took to the stands to attend a Mass and hopefully get a glimpse of Audrey. She arrived in an ambulance and was moved into a small building that had been specially constructed on the grass field. A large window in one wall of the tiny air-conditioned building offered visitors a view of Audrey. The window was made of bulletproof glass—a precaution against tragedy in a decade of terrorist violence and a year when school shootings across the country, from Springfield, Oregon, to Edinboro, Pennsylvania, were making headlines every few weeks.

Among the thousands of pilgrims visiting that day were more than fifty priests, gathered to witness a girl who may possibly be a worker of miracles, a victim soul participating in the Passion of Christ for humanity's benefit. Each visitor was also able to see the Eucharist miracles associated with Audrey Santo: four consecrated Communion hosts upon which blood had mysteriously appeared during Mass in the Santo home. The hosts were placed on an altar that stood next to the building housing Audrey.

Attendance at the annual gatherings for Audrey had been increasing dramatically. In 1996 Audrey's anniversary day was celebrated at a Mass at Christ the King Church with about eight hundred people attending. The next year the event was held in the same place, but word had spread about Audrey Santo. Approximately four thousand pilgrims made their way to the church that day, prompting the large stadium plans for 1998.

The football stadium display—as well as the flow of visitors who for years had journeyed to the Santo home to file past a window looking into Audrey's bedroom—did not sit well with every observer. The Reverend Father F. Stephen Pedone, an expert in canon law for the Worcester diocese who is overseeing the local Audrey Santo investigation, was very honest about his uneasy initial reaction to what he saw in the home. "I was uncomfortable," he told a *Washington Post* reporter about his visit there. "The house was filled with people. A little girl was on display in a bed. One priest was bending over her, whispering intercessions in her ear. . . . My impression was that it bordered on the bizarre. It seemed like an invasion of her privacy."[3] Bishop Daniel Reilly of the Worcester diocese has also expressed regret over the public viewings of the girl, stating that "it turns the girl into a spectacle."[4]

With an attitude that reflects the Church's healthy skepticism of miraculous claims, Father Pedone offered an analysis of why thousands flock to places like South Flagg Street. He reflected that people are desperate for reassurance, and reassurance is good. "The downside is, if the faith lacks basis, it is going to quickly evaporate. The Church is looking for more long-term faith." Father Pedone believes that in a more perfect world, people would be more receptive to the miracles that abound in everyday life and would not be so eager to seek out the extraordinary. "We wake up in the morning," he said. "That is a miracle."[5]

*　　*　　*

With a blanket pulled up to her chin, Audrey's hands and feet were completely hidden from view on Anniversary Day in 1999. Even if visitors were curious about reports that she suffers from the stigmata and bleeds from several places on her body, it wasn't possible to see any traces of the phenomenon that day. According to Linda, Audrey has suffered the stigmata more than fifty times. "Audrey is like a twelfth-century mystic," said Linda. "She's in bed. She's an invalid. And she suffers the total Passion."[6]

In the history of the Church, a number of devout people who have reached states of spiritual ecstasy have also experienced the emotional and physical sufferings of Christ, including the appearance of wounds on their bodies. According to *The Catholic Encyclopedia*, "Many ecstatics bear on hands, feet, side, or brow the marks of the Passion of Christ with corresponding and intense sufferings. These are called visible stigmata. Others only have the sufferings, without any outward marks, and these phenomena are called invisible stigmata."[7] The word is derived from the Greek *stigma*, meaning "mark or brand," which referred in antiquity to the brands made on livestock and slaves. In the fifth century B.C. the

Greek historian Herodotus used the term to describe tattoos placed on people's bodies as a practice of various ancient religions. In medieval times Christian writers and preachers began to focus on the benefits of contemplating Christ's sufferings. In the earliest centuries of the faith, the focus had centered more upon "Christ's triumph over the kingdom of evil."[8] In the Middle Ages, with a new devotion to the sufferings of Christ, stigmata appeared for the first time as actual physical wounds that reflected the devotee's complete participation in Christ's Passion. Pope John Paul II has described the stigmata as a sign and proof of one's identification with Christ. Referring to Padre Pio, a stigmatic whom he knew personally and beatified in 1999, the pope declared that the Capuchin priest had been "a living image of the suffering and resurrected Christ."[9]

Twentieth-century stigmatics like Padre Pio—and possibly Audrey Santo—bring people into contact with a mystery that has had an emotional impact on believers for more than seven hundred years. People believe they are witnessing Christ's suffering, torn from the printed page of the Gospels and experienced in a living person. The medieval centuries produced mystics who stressed meditating on the dramatic scenes and bloody crucifixion of Christ the man. This emphasis coincided with a proliferation of personal religious artifacts that the devotee could use to help focus on the various stages of Christ's Passion. Rather than contemplating the resurrected, triumphant Christ, medieval Christianity dwelled upon the physical, vulnerable, suffering Jesus. Along with this trend came a growing interest in the lives of the saints, in religious places, and in icons and holy relics such as the

Shroud of Turin, which appeared in the mid-1300s. The shroud is thought to be the burial garment of Jesus and bears the stains of his wounds from the crucifixion—a powerful relic in a time when the stigmata were one of the fruits of religious ecstasy. The significance of the body of Christ, as given to his followers at the Last Supper, was glorified in 1264 with the institution of a new feast day, the Feast of Corpus Christi.

One of the most popular spiritual books to grow out of medieval Europe was Thomas à Kempis's *Imitation of Christ*, written in 1426, which details a type of piety based on contemplating Jesus the man rather than on more abstract ideas of God:

> If you cannot [meditate], because of your frailty, always occupy your mind in contemplation of the Godhead, yet be occupied with a remembrance of His Passion, and make for yourself a dwelling place in His blessed wounds. And if you flee devoutly to the wound in Christ's side, and to the marks of His Passion, you will feel great comfort in every trouble.[10]

Some of the mystical experiences included physical suffering that came about at the mere mention of Christ's Passion. Margaretha Ebner, a nun in Medingen, Germany, who died in 1351, had frequent episodes of paralysis while "in the grip of a divine joy."[11] At first this state was brought on by listening to descriptions of Christ's suffering, but eventually she went into a nearly catatonic state after simply hearing Jesus' name. A significant theme among the cloistered nuns of the time was that of meeting Christ in the form of the divine child or the divine bridegroom. Margaretha Ebner kept a cradle in her cell in which she imagined the baby Jesus unable to sleep, whom she would have to take lovingly into her arms. In an essay on life in the fourteenth and fifteenth centuries, Philippe Braunstein writes: "Women lavished devoted attention on wood or plaster images of the Virgin and dreamed of giving birth to Christ; such identification stemmed from religious instruction based on immersion in Bible stories." He also notes that Christ frequently appeared as a young child to nuns in the late fourteenth century, prompting a traditional dialogue: " 'Who is your father,' they would ask upon seeing a child in the cloister. *'Pater noster!'* the child would answer and then disappear."[12]

The actual number of stigmatics throughout Church history is not known, although one major study published in the late nineteenth century claims that there have been 321. In 1894 French scholar and physician A. Imbert-Gourbeyre published a two-volume catalog of stigmatics entitled *La Stigmatisation*. Theologians do not universally credit Dr. Imbert-Gourbeyre with excellent scholarship, however, and the *New Catholic Encyclopedia* claims that the work has "serious defects."[13] Nevertheless, by compiling this list, the author created a useful trail of exploration into a phenomenon that is difficult to verify. Of the 321 stigmatics on this list, only forty-one are men. Most have been Catholics, but there are a handful of Anglicans and other Protestants on the contemporary list, too. The phenomenon is not limited to Christianity, however: according to Ian Wilson's book on the stigmata entitled *The Bleeding Mind,* there are stories of Moslems who have manifested wounds associated with their spiritual leader, Muhammad. The prophet was tortured, beaten, and stoned by his enemies at various times in his life, and these types of wounds have reportedly appeared on some of his followers.[14]

According to Dr. Imbert-Gourbeyre's book, and also well accepted by Church historians, the first person to receive the mystical stigmata was Saint Francis of Assisi (1182–1226). There is also a theory that the apostle Paul had received the stigmata, as revealed in his letter to the Galatians: "I carry branded on my body the marks of Jesus" (Galatians 6:17). Paul's message of imitating Christ, suffering for Christ, and identifying with Christ to the point of "being molded to the pattern of his death" (Philippians 3:10) has made him a strong candidate as a stigmatist in the minds of many theologians, but the Church has not officially recognized him as such.

Saint Francis received the mystical wounds during an astonishing vision on a mountaintop. Fifteen years after establishing his own order, Francis retired from his intensely active life of religious service and went to Mount Alverna for a period of isolated prayer and contemplation of Christ and his suffering. Ever since his conversion when Jesus spoke to him from a crucifix, Francis had been deeply committed to contemplating Christ's Passion. Before sunrise on the morning of September 14, 1224, Francis was praying in front of his hut on Mount Alverna. He faced east so he would be able to greet the first rays of the sun and extended his arms to the sky. Sensing that he did not have long to live, he prayed:

O Lord Jesus Christ, two favors I beg of thee before I die. The first is, that I may, as far as it is possible, feel in my soul and in my body the suffering which thou, O gentle Jesus, sustained in the bitter passion. And the second favor is, that I, as far as it is possible, may receive into my heart that excessive charity by which thou, the son of God, wast inflamed.[15]

As he prayed, Francis felt an inner certainty that God would grant him his wishes. He meditated on the sufferings and love of Jesus and went into a rapturous state. In his vision he saw an angel come down from the sky with three pairs of wings, and as it got closer, he could see that it was Jesus crucified on a cross. The Lord revealed to him that the vision had been given to him so that he would understand that "it was not by bodily martyrdom, but through an inner flame, that he should be transformed entirely into the likeness of Christ the Crucified."[16]

After the vision faded, the marks of the crucifixion began to appear on Francis's body, in the form of the nails themselves rather than the bloody wounds that would eventually be most often associated with stigmata. The round, black head of a nail appeared on his palms and on the top of his feet, the points of these nails protruding from the other side. There was also a bleeding wound on his left side in the place where Jesus was pierced by the soldier's sword. The stigmata remained with Saint Francis until he died, two years later, on October 3, 1226.

Of the hundreds of stigmatics on record, sixty-two have been blesseds or saints like Saint Francis, including Saint

Teresa of Ávila. Her invisible stigmata took the form of a mysterious wound to the heart called *transverberation*, or the Wound of Love. In a vision she saw an angel holding a golden dart with a tip that was on fire. The angel thrust this dart into her several times, and when he finally withdrew, Teresa felt that he had taken away part of her to leave more room for God: "I thought that he was carrying off with him the deepest part of me; and he left me all on fire with great love of God."[17] Her body exuded a sweet fragrance that is associated with many mystics as well as with the presence of the Blessed Virgin Mary. This scent intensified after Saint Teresa's death, to the point that the nuns had to open the windows and door to her cell; it also emanated from her when her body was exhumed nine months later, and again three years later when she was reburied at the convent in Alba de Tormes in Spain. Her body at that time was still incorrupt (not decayed), and her heart was removed and placed in a crystal case that is on view to this day in the convent. The heart is reported to carry a scar where Saint Teresa received the wound from the angel's dart.

Another saint who received the stigmata, both visible and invisible, was Saint Catherine of Siena (1347–80). After receiving the bleeding wounds, she prayed to Jesus to have them taken away, and he granted her request. The internal pain and suffering of the stigmata remained throughout her life, and the visible marks returned just before she died. Like Saint Teresa of Ávila who would follow two centuries later, Saint Catherine experienced levitation during her periods of mystical union with God. She experienced Christ removing her heart with his hands and, days later, opening her side again and placing his own heart inside her. In another visionary experience she was given a jewel-encrusted gold ring that marked her sacred marriage with Jesus, although she was the only one who could see it. The finger on which she wore this ring, which is still uncorrupted, has been saved as a holy relic and is kept in a reliquary in the Cathedral of Saints Catherine and Dominic in Siena, Italy.

Another Italian stigmatic who is remembered for her divine marriage with Christ is Saint Catherine dei Ricci (1522–90). At age twenty, Catherine began a series of weekly sufferings of the Passion that began on Thursday and ended on Friday at four o'clock in the afternoon. Her suffering included the Five Sacred Wounds; bleeding wounds on the hands, feet, and side; she also received bleeding marks on her head where Christ wore the crown of thorns.

According to Linda Santo and some of Audrey's caregivers, Audrey's stigmata also follow the days and hours of the week associated with Christ's suffering.

Like Saint Catherine, St. Veronica Giuliani of Urbino, Italy (1660–1727), received the stigmata in the form of bleeding wounds on Christ's crown of thorns. A novice mistress in the order of Poor Clares, her bleeding wounds prompted the local bishop to order her to have medical treatment, but the doctor could not help her. When she was only four years old, Saint Veronica's dying mother had entrusted each of her five daughters to one of the Five Sacred Wounds. To Veronica she entrusted the wound just below Jesus' heart, where he was pierced. The mother's dying wish came true on Good Friday in 1697, when Veronica was thirty-seven years old. She felt a strong desire to participate in Christ's Passion and suddenly received an excruciating physical pain in her heart. Some time after her death, her body was exhumed, and her heart was found to be incorrupt and marked with an impression of a cross.

Born forty-seven years after the death of Saint Veronica, Venerable Anne Catherine Emmerich (1774–1824) of Germany became another renowned ecstatic and stigmatic. Her wounds began as severe pain in her hands, feet, and side, followed by visible stigmata, which eventually also bled from her head. Just before she received the visible stigmata, Venerable Anne received another physical imprint on her body: a cross-shaped wound on her chest above her heart. Since early childhood Anne had experienced frequent visions of Jesus and Mary and spoke daily with her guardian angel. When sick people visited her, she automatically knew their diseases and how to treat them (a man who became famous for this ability in the twentieth century was the American Edgar Cayce). Seven years after receiving the visible stigmata, Anne prayed to have the wounds removed, and her prayer was granted as the marks gradually disappeared. The blood began to flow again, however, during each Lenten season and during various holy days on the Church calendar. Even when the stigmata did not appear on her body, she continued to suffer pain in those areas.

Anne Emmerich spent many hours of the day in ecstasy, traveling to other realms with her guardian angel, wrestling with demons, receiving visions of the saints, and hearing prophecies. She described this other reality as much brighter and more real than the ordinary world, calling it a place where "nothing hinders one, not time, nor space, nor body, nor secrecy, where everything speaks and everything shines, seems so perfect and free that this blind, lame, stammering reality seems like an empty dream in it."[18] From the neighbors and pilgrims who came to visit her to the church officials who examined her, everyone who came into contact with Anne Emmerich was touched by the special aura of sanctity that surrounded her. Other creatures in the natural world responded to her, too, just as they had with the first stigmatic, Saint Francis of Assisi: "When I worked in the garden," Anne Emmerich said, "the birds came to me, sat on my head and shoulders, and we sang praises to God together."[19]

A well-documented stigmatic whose wounds appeared only on the surface of her side, hands, feet, and head—without breaking the skin—was Louise Lateau (1850–83), a woman from Belgium. During the last fifteen years of her short life, Louise suffered from the stigmata every Friday. She was thoroughly examined by medical doctors, officials from the Catholic Church, and psychologists, none of whom could find any medical reason for the spontaneous appearance of the blood on her body. On Fridays devoted pilgrims sat at Louise's bedside, wiping away the blood with handkerchiefs and cloth. One such bloodstained cloth, a piece of linen, is in the religious archives of the University of Notre Dame in Indiana. Louise Lateau also experienced a mystical grace known as *inedia,* or not eating. It is reported that for twelve years she ate nothing but a Communion wafer every day, and three or four glasses of water per week. The physical pain that Louise Lateau felt during the appearance of the stigmata on Fridays persisted every day of the week, eventually preventing her from leaving her home to attend Mass.

Another well-chronicled stigmatic was born in the twentieth century, with the profuse bleeding of her stigmata captured on film and in photographs. Therese Neumann (1898–1962) was born on Good Friday in a small German town. Her stigmata were of the kind suffered by Saint Francis: rather than openings in the skin or mere bleeding on the surface, they appeared as fleshy, nail-like protrusions that completely penetrated her hands and feet. The marks of her stigmata included the Five Sacred Wounds, the crown of thorns, the shoulder wound where Christ carried the cross, and many scourge marks representing where Christ was whipped before Pilate. She also bled from the eyes, and many photographs exist of two wide streams of blood flowing down Therese's face.

A contemporary of Therese Neumann and perhaps the most renowned stigmatic in Church history after Saint Francis of Assisi was Padre Pio (1887–1968). Born in southern Italy, he took the name of Friar Pio when he entered a Capuchin monastery at age fifteen. The Capuchin order traces its origin back to Saint Francis, and in 1918 Padre Pio was assigned to the Capuchin monastery of San Giovanni Rotondo, where he remained for the rest of his life. In that same year, Padre Pio received the stigmata that he would endure for the next fifty years. After the morning Mass he was sitting alone in the church when he suddenly went into a quiet state that blotted out everything except a profound sense of peace. The crucifix before him transformed into a great light, and flaming shafts of light struck him in the hands and feet. After the light disappeared, he was found lying on the floor, his hands, feet, and left side dripping with blood. The previous month the same "exalted being" (whom he later identified as Christ) had come to him and pierced him in his left side with a sword. He described that first wound as something that caused him agonizing pain: "I cannot tell you how much I suffered during this period of anguish. Even my internal organs were torn and ruptured by that weapon. . . . From that day on I have been mortally wounded. I feel in the depths of my soul a wound that is always open and causes me continual agony."[20] He admitted that although the wounds were always present, his suffering was more intense on Thursday nights and Fridays, the days of the week when Christ endured his final suffering and crucifixion.

Padre Pio's wounds bled for the next five decades, and although he desperately tried to hide the marks on his hands beneath a pair of fingerless gloves, word spread quickly about his visible stigmata as well as the apparent suffering he went through every time he said Mass. Thousands of people have reported that they felt the presence of God at Padre Pio's Mass and came away with a new outlook on the meaning of life. One participant recalled that "as I knelt next to the altar, I could clearly see the suffering Padre Pio was going through from the pain in his wounds. His feet and hands would jerk as if great pain was shooting through his body. He made painful expressions all during the Mass, never noticing anyone in the church. I had the sense that he was physically here but spiritually . . . with Christ at the foot of the cross. At times he wept with tears running down his face, as if he were watching Christ being nailed to the cross."[21]

Padre Pio's stigmata was thoroughly investigated by medical doctors during the course of his life, and the wounds were not found to be self-inflicted or from any natural cause. One priest who frequently accompanied Padre Pio in his later years described the bleeding wounds on his hands as "the size and shape of a coin. They were covered with a crust of dried blood. . . . Once the crust would start to break, it would form sharp projections that pointed into his flesh and would be very painful."[22]

In the Santo family's home chapel there is a large photograph of Padre Pio saying Mass, and the dark traces of the stigmata can be seen around the edges of his gloves. Oil is continuously flowing from this photograph and staining the wall beneath it.

Throughout his life Padre Pio suffered from many illnesses but never gave up his commitment to a life of prayer and service. Today the small town of San Giovanni where Padre Pio lived and built a hospital is visited by 7 million pilgrims a year. Six hundred thousand people thronged into St. Peter's Square in May 1999 for the ceremony in which Pope John Paul II beatified Padre Pio, making him a "blessed" servant of God, one step away from sainthood. The pope had known of Padre Pio since his days as a young priest, as he had once made his confession to the friar. Later, when the Polish priest became a bishop, he wrote Padre Pio to ask him to pray for a friend, a mother of four, who was very ill with cancer. The woman's tumor mysteriously disappeared after this request, and the doctors were dumbfounded.

During the beatification ceremony, the pope said that Padre Pio was "a living image of the suffering and resurrected Christ" and that the stigmata were a proof of the friar's identification with Christ.[23] Father Fidel Gonzales, a

Vatican official, described Padre Pio as "a new Saint Francis, gifted with the very same charisma. He brought the charisma of Saint Francis nearer to our day. . . . His suffering itself had clearly a missionary dimension, since the suffering of Christ is a redeeming suffering, for the salvation of all mankind. . . . He realized that he was completing the Lord's Passion for the good of the Church."[24]

A few months before Padre Pio's death, the deep wounds of his stigmata suddenly disappeared without leaving any trace of scarring. This was the final miraculous event in the life of a man who had been the source of thousands of miraculous healings, who reportedly read the souls of some who came to him for confession before they had a chance to speak, who spoke to his guardian angel daily like a brother and wrestled with demons in clashes that woke up the rest of the monastery. As described by the Vatican, Padre Pio was "a religious absorbed in the supernatural realities."[25]

Audrey Santo, whose stigmata have been witnessed by her family and caregivers, is in the company of several stigmatics at the dawn of the twenty-first century. Christina Gallagher, a housewife from County Mayo in northwestern Ireland, is experiencing the stigmata in addition to receiving messages from the Virgin Mary. The stigmata bring her much pain, and many people have witnessed the bleeding wounds in her feet. Christina explains that "the marks—the stigmata—have bled at times. It's as if a great heat comes from them. They get raw and then go away. I have pain from the marks when they're visible, although I sometimes have the pain even more severely without the marks showing at all."[26] A visiting Irish priest observed that "the wounded limbs of the Crucified are, as it were, replicated in her body, and the thorn-makers stand out starkly on her forehead. The suffering she undergoes is agonizing; yet she offers it readily, indeed almost eagerly, in reparation for the sins of the world—especially the sins of the world's priests."[27]

On the other side of the world, a Korean woman has been receiving the stigmata and messages from Mary since the mid-1980s. Julia Kim lives in Naju, a small town on the southwestern tip of the Korean peninsula. After experiencing a vision of the crucified Christ, she felt moved to ask Jesus to allow her to share his suffering. After that prayer she began to experience physical pain and eventually exhibited the bleeding, visible stigmata. Like several other stigmatics throughout history, she asked that the visible marks be taken away because "they attract too much attention from others."[28] In Julia's case the request was granted. She continues to feel pain, but her stigmata are no longer visible. Julia's Marian visitations and other supernatural events—such as the stigmata and bleeding Communion hosts and statues—have drawn many pilgrims to the small town, and the Virgin Mary is known there as Our Lady of Naju.

In a Christian neighborhood of Damascus in Syria, a young woman received the stigmata four times between 1983 and 1990. Mary Kourbet Al-Akhras, the daughter of Greek Catholic and Orthodox parents, has bled from the hands, feet, side, and head. This woman, who is married with two children, has received visitations from Mary and experienced several mystical events, such as a constant flow of oil from her hands when she prays.

Catalina Rivas of Cochabamba, Bolivia, came to the attention of Americans in the 1990s through a Fox network television program. She had already published books containing messages to her from Mary and Jesus when she received the stigmata during a visit to the Marian apparition site in Conyers, Georgia. Catalina's description of the experience is reminiscent of that of Saint Francis and Padre Pio. As she knelt before the crucifix on the hill, she saw a bright light around the figure of Jesus and felt a strong need to offer her life to him. "Two very strong lights came out of the hands of my Lord and I felt like a lightning bolt had gone through my own hands," she said. "I felt the strong pain, and then a light came out of His feet, and it came to my own feet; the light split in two to my two feet. The third light came out of His side, it went straight to my heart, and there I fell to the ground because the pain was too strong."[29] Later, after her return to Bolivia, the stigmata became visible, and one of her dramatic Thursday-to-Friday episodes was captured on film by an Australian production company as well as by Fox.

A priest in the Washington, D.C., area became headline news in the early 1990s when statues began weeping in his church and he received the stigmata. Father James Bruse was an associate pastor at the St. Elizabeth Ann Seton Church in Lake Ridge, Virginia, when a statue in his room began flowing with blood and he received the stigmata on his wrists and feet. He showed his wounds to his superior, Father Daniel Hamilton, who has since seen Father James's stigmata several times. "Of course I doubted it in the beginning," said Father Hamilton, "and then I saw some of this stuff he'd been talking about. It's true. That's all I can tell you. It's true. It's true."[30] Father James moved to another parish in 1995 and is now the very busy pastor of two churches in Kilmarnock, Virginia. The stigmata and the weeping statues stopped before he moved to his new parish. Although Father Bruse is mystified by the events, he knows they served a purpose. "Everything quieted down," he told a reporter in 1997. "But the result was conversions and stronger faith. It strengthened people's faith. It brought a lot of people back to God. Those are its fruits after those years. I'm still seeing that from the letters and phone calls."[31]

Audrey Santo joined this company of modern-day stigmatics when she was five years old, and like many of them before her, she usually receives the wounds during Holy Week. Her first episode reportedly began during the Lenten season of 1989. At noon on Good Friday her nurse noticed that the girl suddenly became rigid, with her shoulders back and her chest thrust forward. Audrey's pulse and heart rate shot up, and her palms became red. The skin began to peel and looked severely chaffed until it formed open creases and sores that began to bleed. Afterward the sores closed up as mysteriously as they had appeared. The nurse, Sonia Huerta, R.N., was keenly aware that Audrey seemed to be in intense pain, her face contorted into expressions of suffering "like she was agonizing."[32]

This was the beginning of what would become a frequent terrifying experience for everyone near Audrey. Her family and medical caregivers looked on, unable to do anything to relieve her suffering, as Audrey went into a rigid state and bled from fresh wounds in her hands, feet, side, and head. Another of Audrey's nurses, Joanne Erickson, witnessed the creases in the girl's palms splitting open and bleeding during Holy Week of 1992. Audrey also manifested "marks on top of her feet, on her sides, and on her forehead" as the nurse watched. The unexplained marks on her forehead were in the form of purple streaks that zigzagged across her brow.[33]

"Her Passion is inside and out," explained Linda Santo. "Our Lord died of asphyxiation. If I had a pulse rate of two hundred for eight hours, I would be dead. Audrey isn't. When Audrey comes back to us, she's actually quite well. We would be very weak and very sick, and that's why what God's doing is not of this world, [it's] a divine type of suffering."[34]

The wounds in Audrey's feet and hands would appear and disappear suddenly, sometimes having lingered for days at a time, usually from Thursday through Sunday. The Santo family and her caregivers have also seen streaky, slashlike bruises all over her body that mirror the marks made when Jesus was whipped. Images of doves would rise up like welts on top of her hands, much like the marks of crosses and other symbols that have appeared on the bodies of mystics throughout history. During some episodes in 1998, when Audrey was rigid and her back arched, she could not be lifted even though she weighed only about thirty pounds. Linda believes this is another sign of God's grace in Audrey's life, the unusual "phenomenon of weight," when the laws of nature are suspended and a body is too heavy to move. While she was in this rigid, immovable posture, Audrey's eyes were open and her pulse was racing. To Linda, she appeared to be "in what mystical theologians call ecstasy."[35] During Lent in 1989 Audrey wept uncontrollably, and neither her nurses nor her family could find anything that would physically account for her suffering. Her face was puffy and red from crying day after day. Then, at exactly three P.M. on Good Friday, she stopped crying and went into a deep sleep. This is commonly regarded as the time when Jesus died on the cross. Audrey repeated this suffering in subsequent years during Holy Week, and Linda has reported that her experience of the Passion also includes bleeding from her nose, ears, mouth, and through her tracheostomy tube. After her suffering on a Thursday night and Friday, she usually falls asleep until Sunday. According to Linda, this has happened "many, many, many times. It's all documented."[36] (To date, none of this documentation has been released to the public.) Linda also claims that this documentation shows that Audrey sometimes stops breathing when her suffering stops abruptly on a Friday afternoon.

Audrey Santo's mysterious wounds and unusual physical experiences echo the events of Christianity's long lineage of stigmatics. One of the fundamental aspects of the stigmata is the suffering that goes on beneath the surface, the pain that endures with or without the appearance of blood. Although Audrey cannot speak about her suffering, those close to her—who feel connected to her in a bond that is deeper than language—are convinced that she is in agony during these episodes.

Is there a point to such suffering? According to the stories of many mystics throughout the centuries, there is a deep, significant meaning. Scattered throughout classic spiritual writings by mystics and biographies of contemporary stigmatics such as Padre Pio are expressions of the privilege of sharing the suffering of Christ, to add fuel to the redemptive

Left: *Since 1998, visiting time at the chapel in the Santo home has been limited to four hours per day, three days per week. The chapel is located inside the garage connected to the house.* (ANTONIA FELIX)

Below: *Visitors wait in line to see Audrey inside Christ the King Church on August 9, 1999. About five thousand visitors filed through the church that day to get a glimpse of Audrey behind a window. These "Pilgrim Days," celebrated annually on the anniversary of Audrey's near-drowning accident, draw thousands of pilgrims to Worcester, Massachusetts.* (ANTONIA FELIX)

power of his suffering. This concept of gladly and enthusiastically volunteering to suffer for the sake of others is at the heart of the life of the victim soul. Many believe that Audrey Santo has chosen or accepted this role for herself and that each day of her life has been part of a divine plan that is unfolding with enormous consequences throughout the world.

4.

Strange Paths: The Sufferer and Victim Soul

God guides his chosen children along strange paths. This is a strange path and a noble path and a holy path that God himself trod: that a human being, though free of sin and guilt, suffer pain. Upon this path the soul that aches for God is joyful, for by nature she is joyful to her Lord, who suffered much pain because of his good deeds.
— Mechthild of Magdeburg (1208–c. 1282)[1]

Suffer with Christ and for Christ if you wish to reign with Him. — Thomas à Kempis

To suffer lovingly is to suffer no longer. — Saint John Vianney

Many people, including Linda Santo and several priests close to the family, believe that Audrey is a victim soul, a person chosen by God to suffer for the benefit of humanity. Author Kevin Orlin Johnson, Ph.D., defines a victim soul as "an innocent person who's called to emulate the mission of Christ himself: a person who's asked by God to suffer torments of reparation for the sins of others and accepts."[2] He goes on to make a distinction between an illness that may come up while cleansing the soul and the illness of the true victim soul—which is a gift. The victim soul is separate and apart, specially chosen by God for a high purpose.

Was Audrey Santo's life preordained by God to include her drowning accident and all the physical suffering that she has endured since then? Is she, lying silent and unmoving in her bed, offering herself in some mysterious way to offset a nuclear bombing attack on civilians in Japan, as one priest believes? Did she communicate with the Virgin Mary in the Medjugorje apparition room and offer her life at that moment as a victim soul? Does she embrace her inability to speak, eat, or breathe fully on her own with a pious heart? Is she living her life out of body, whispering people's prayers into Jesus' ear while her helpless body lies on the bed? Or is she completely unaware of her circumstances, unable to comprehend anyone or anything, yet meticulously loved and cared for in a home that inspires everyone who has visited her?

These questions address the deepest mysteries about Audrey Santo as expressed by her family members and the priests who are close to them. They believe that her present physical condition is just one aspect of a holy life that has been dedicated to God since before her birth. They believe that her suffering is part of a grand plan to bring both physical and spiritual healing to others. They are convinced that Audrey has been specially chosen by God as a victim soul to do his work. This portrait of Audrey's life gives spiritual meaning to her suffering and draws comparisons to some of the most beloved mystics and saints in Christian history.

The lives of the mystics were ridden with illness and suffering, both physical and spiritual. They rarely enjoyed robust health, buckling under the turmoils that battled inside them. The thirteenth-century Beguine Mechthild of Magdeburg, a traveler on one of God's "strange paths," was severely sick throughout her life and was blind in her final years. The Beguines, women and men who chose to live cloistered lives outside of traditional Catholic orders, pledged themselves to lives of poverty, chastity, prayer, and service to the community. The movement was strong in Germany and other parts of northern Europe in the thirteenth century—which Mechthild's lifetime nearly spanned—but gradually dissolved in the face of church opposition. The Beguines, like other religious reformers, sought a simpler religious life that reflected the lives of the apostles and the early Church. Such austerity helped remove the worldly obstacles that hide the soul from God. Mechthild's books were both popular and controversial in her day, partly because she was relatively uneducated and wrote in German rather than in Latin, which was more respected in the scholarly religious world. Mechthild described her writings as holy, sublime contemplations received directly from the Holy Spirit.

As with so many mystics who came before and after her, suffering played a central role in Mechthild's personal life, a suffering that cleansed and had other redemptive qualities. One of the messages she received explained, in no uncertain terms, the purpose of her various sufferings: "As I," she wrote, "in my disloyalty, was being ill-tempered because of my suffering, God gave me this consolation and said: 'Look, no one can do without suffering because it purifies a person of his many sins from hour to hour.'"

Another important theme among the mystics has been the saving power of suffering, the belief that one can merge with Christ's suffering and be a co-savior with him for the benefit of all people. Linda Santo, who compares her daughter with the saints throughout history, believes that this is the purpose of Audrey's suffering.

Mechthild envisioned this suffering relationship as a way to tip the scales in Christ's favor at the end of the world:

> On the last day, Christ Jesus shall hold aloft a glorious scale before his Father. Upon it will lie his holy toil and his innocent suffering, and in it and next to it all the blameless torment, humiliation, and interior pain that was ever suffered by human beings for the love of Christ.[3]

States of mystical ecstasy could lift a physical body from the floor—or send it crashing down in an unbearable fit of anguish. In a thirteenth-century collection of writings by sisters from a German convent, Sofia von Klingnau wrote about the deep regret that took hold of her during prayer one day. Realizing how much she had neglected the "dignified treasure of my noble soul," she was filled with torment that caused her "physical suffering and pain, as if my heart had a physical wound." After a few moments of this, she tried to stand up but "fell down with no control over myself and fell into a swoon, so that I could neither see nor hear nor speak."[4]

Mystics have also described the agonizing spiritual suffering that comes with longing to be closer to God. Saint Teresa of Ávila, writing of her soul's yearning for Christ in the form of the beloved spouse, experiences "great grief" when her soul "realizes that He is present but will not manifest Himself in such a way as to allow it to enjoy Him."[5] Another significant form of mystical suffering comes when the soul is purged of its imperfections, one of the steps on the journey toward union with God. This type of suffering brings on the "dark night of the soul" as described by sixteenth-century Spanish mystic Saint John of the Cross.

From Saint Paul to Padre Pio to many of today's stigmatics, suffering for others is one of the main purposes of the mystic's life. The saints were asked, in visionary experiences, to take part in Christ's suffering, or they requested it on their own, often feeling powerfully compelled to ask this of God. The acceptance of this burden often led directly to suffering in spirit and body. Spiritual suffering precedes a physical manifestation, just as the invisible stigmata always come before the visible, if the bleeding wounds appear at all. Sharing in Christ's Passion with one's entire being as a victim soul is considered a blessing, a gift from God, something only a special chosen few are called to do. Saint Paul offered his body and soul as a sacrifice to continue Christ's mission on earth: "It makes me happy to be suffering for you now, and in my own body to make up all the hardships that still have to be undergone by Christ for the sake of his body, the Church, of which I was made a servant with the responsibility towards you that God gave to me."[6]

In the *Interior Castle*, Saint Teresa of Ávila asks her sisters to

embrace the Cross which your Spouse bore upon His shoulders and realize that this Cross is yours to carry too: let her who is capable of the greatest suffering suffer most for Him and she will have the most perfect freedom. All other things are of quite secondary importance: if the Lord should grant them to you, give Him heartfelt thanks.[7]

A victim soul who cheerfully endured wretched physical suffering and consequently brought about many conversions was Blessed Lydwine of Schiedam (1380–1433). At age seven she dedicated herself to God, hoping to become a nun one day. Her parents had hoped to eventually marry her into a good family, but a series of illnesses and accidents took her out of the running before it became an issue. Her first sickness was smallpox, which left her skin scarred and damaged. Then she broke her right rib in an ice-skating accident, and it never healed properly and confined her to the sickbed—which she would not leave for the next forty years. A tumor grew on the girl's wounded rib and burst inside her one day, starting a gangrenous infection that led to a infiltration of worms inside her body. This was just the beginning of Lydwine's suffering, which she accepted in stride because she believed that her survival was for the glory of God. She fell victim to two plagues, one of which ate away at her shoulder until her right arm was left dangling by just one tendon. Her organs decayed, her skin burst, and she was literally held together by strips of cloth and pillows. Through it all, a sweet fragrance poured from her infected wounds and she amazed her constant round of visitors with her sense of humor and tireless devotion to God. Pilgrims from all over Europe came to visit the girl whose body rotted yet stayed alive and to see for themselves her supernatural gifts, such as the stigmata and her ability to read into a person's soul. There are many more horrible ailments that befell Lydwine, but most important is that this lifelong invalid "bore the pain as reparation for the sins of others."[8] Since childhood Lydwine volunteered her life and suffering for the sake of humankind.

Like Lydwine, Audrey Santo suffers from a tragic physical condition that arouses the curiosity and, in some cases, deepens the faith of those who believe she is following a divine plan. Accepting or volunteering for the role of victim soul is an important part of this personal sacrifice. Some victim souls offer themselves with specific intentions, asking to be used as a counteractive measure against evil events in the world. Padre Pio renewed his offering as a victim soul in July 1918, in the hope of ending the war. "No sooner had I made this offering," he wrote to his spiritual director, Padre Benedetto, "than I felt myself plunged into a terrible prison and heard the crash of the gate behind me."[9] One month later he received the vision in which Christ pierced his side, giving him his first invisible stigmata. Padre Pio had endured years of suffering before this specific request, and he often wrote to his spiritual director for comfort and guidance. Padre Benedetto was aware of Padre Pio's voluntary suffering and once told him, "The Omnipotent wants to make a holocaust of you."[10]

One of the Church's newest saints, Edith Stein, offered herself specifically as a sacrifice for world peace just before the outbreak of World War II. Born into a devout Jewish family, she became a distinguished philosopher and decided to convert to Christianity after reading Saint Teresa of Ávila's autobiography, becoming a Carmelite nun at age forty-two. Drawn to Teresa's message of suffering and becoming one with Christ's suffering, she took the name Sister Teresa Benedicta of the Cross. As the Jews in Germany were being beaten and driven from their homes on the orders of Adolf Hitler in 1938, Edith asked God to use her life to atone for the horrors that surrounded her. "I firmly believe that the Lord has accepted my life as an offering for all," she wrote that year. Even though she was uncertain about her role during this dark time, she trusted in her deep bond with God and the responsibility that went with it. "I know . . . what it means to be betrothed to the Lord in the sign of the Cross," she wrote. "But it's not something that can ever be understood. It is a mystery."[11] After fleeing Germany to Holland, Edith wrote to her mother superior in the spring of 1939:

> Please permit me to offer myself to the Heart of Jesus as a sacrifice of atonement for true peace, that if possible the reign of Antichrist might be broken without another world war and a new social order might be established. . . . I know I myself am nothing, but Jesus desires it, and I am sure he is asking it of many others in these days.[12]

Edith Stein was rounded up with fellow Jewish converts to Christianity during World War II and was killed at Auschwitz. Pope John Paul II declared her a saint in 1998, calling her "an eminent daughter of Israel and a faithful daughter of the Church."[13]

The current-day visionary and stigmatic Christina Gallagher has described the victim soul as a person who opens her body and soul to let God work through it. If humanity is all part of the body of Christ, the victim soul is like a living, open hand that is ready to do God's work, according to Gallagher. A person who doesn't believe in God is like a paralyzed, useless limb in the body of Christ. Gallagher believes that someone who responds to God helps compensate for the unbelievers and allows God's love to flow into the world. The person who is open to God, who dedicates her heart and soul to God, is a living part of God's work:

> God can then pour His grace into this person's soul. So, the person's heart is open to respond to God's spirit and grace. . . . The more God gives to this open person, the more the Evil One wants to attack him because of his value to the Mystical Body of Christ. This is what Jesus does through the surrender and suffering of the victim soul. . . . Anyone who loves Jesus will love suffering because Jesus draws good out of suffering for the conversion of others.[14]

Saint Paul, Padre Pio, Edith Stein, and contemporary mystics like Christina Gallagher are all examples of those who willingly offered themselves as living sacrifices for God's work. Audrey Santo has not been able to make this declaration with words, but her family believes that she has so offered herself. In the doctrine of the Church, the very concept of the victim soul is a controversial issue. The Worcester diocese's report on Bishop Reilly's initial investigation into Audrey emphasizes that using this terminology puts us on shaky ground:

> More systematic study must be done before the Church can even begin to evaluate the concept of "victim soul," which has been applied to Audrey. We must proceed quite cautiously here, since this term is not commonly used by the Church except for Christ himself who became the victim for our sins and transgressions on the cross.[15]

Audrey's ability to willingly accept the role of victim soul is as controversial as the concept itself. Father George Joyce, one of Audrey's spiritual directors, believes that Audrey gave her consent while in Medjugorje with her mother. In the apparition room on those two hot evenings in July 1988, the visionary Ivan Dragicevic spoke to Audrey quietly in Croatian. No one but Ivan knows what he told her, but when Linda described the scenes to Father Joyce, he was convinced that Audrey made a connection with Ivan and the Blessed Virgin, communicating to them her consent to become a victim soul. Father Joyce is very familiar with the special environment of Medjugorje, and because of the miraculous events that began to occur around Audrey upon her return, he believes that something special happened in that apparition room. "It could have been anywhere else," he told author Thomas Petrisko. "But that would be the logical place, because so much is happening over there. It seems that when Audrey was there for the last apparition, I think that was the moment that she accepted the victimhood from our Lord and through Mary."[16]

Having spent years at Audrey's bedside, Father Joyce is convinced that her purpose on earth is to suffer for the sake of others. "Either she's a fake," he said, "the greatest one that I've ever met, or she's a genuine victim soul."[17]

Father Emmanuel McCarthy holds another view concerning Audrey's consent to become a victim soul. He doesn't see any need for discussion on where, when, or how Audrey was capable of making such a choice after her accident, because he believes she offered her life in this way when she received the sacrament of baptism. "Audrey," he said, "by her baptism, is totally incorporated into Christ. . . . After her baptism, every act of hers is moved out of the Spirit of Christ in whom she totally lives and moves and has her being. . . . Under those circumstances, Jesus can choose Audrey for His purposes, which always includes suffering love."[18]

Like Father George Joyce, Father John Meade has been designated as one of Audrey's spiritual directors. Father Meade believes that Audrey's entire life is the fulfillment of a divine plan in which God has chosen her as a victim soul. He refers to Audrey's drowning in the family pool as a "so-called" accident, viewing it as part of God's design. In his homily at Audrey's anniversary mass at Christ the King Church in August 1996, Father Meade said that he had seen Audrey's face contort into expressions of horror, which revealed that she was viewing souls going to hell. He believes that Audrey is suffering in reparation for the lack of prayer among the faithful. "Because we don't offer up our prayers like we should," he told the gathering that day, "she takes it upon herself, twenty-four hours a day. You see the suffering in her eyes. She willingly, joyfully takes [it] on, because of her great love for the little Jesus. She loves to suffer for him, and she loves to suffer for you and me. She loves it; she feels very much a part of us, very much a part of our life. She's out of the body. She's very seldom in the body."

Father Meade invited those at the Mass to follow Audrey's example and offer their lives and suffering to Christ for the sake of everyone. "We unite our suffering, as Audrey has, with Christ's, with the sorrowful Mother," he said. "For the souls of all of God's children, all his creation, that he literally loves together. . . . Thank you for this great gift of little Audrey."[19]

Linda Santo agrees with Father Meade that Audrey is a victim soul who is living out a divine plan. God's unfolding holy design has been since her birth. "As her family we believe she was chosen before she was born and manifested these things very early on in her life and continues to do this," said Linda. "She does two things: she brings you to Jesus, back to the sacraments, and she's a statement of life in our culture of death." Although she prays for Audrey's recovery every day, Linda also believes that since the accident Audrey has been in a perpetual state of communion with Christ. "She's the only person in the entire world that spends seven days a week, twenty-four hours a day, with our Lord. There is nowhere else, no adoration chapel, nowhere when one person does that." Linda explains that because of this constant love and adoration given to Jesus, the Lord showers

Audrey with graces such as sending oil to flow in the chalices and on the religious images in her home and making the sacred hosts bleed in her tabernacle. Giving more power to her role as a victim soul, in the eyes of both Linda and Father Meade, is the fact that Audrey is perfectly innocent and without sin. "She's a child, she's never sinned," said Linda. "She continues not to commit sin, and this is very important. She's the purest of the victim souls that any of the priests or theologians that have been here know of in the Catholic Church."[20]

Linda's sister, Jeri Cox, added that Audrey has always drawn people to her in a special way, before and after the accident. She also sees Audrey as a person specially chosen by God to fulfill a special plan. "I believe Audrey had this mission to bring you all to Jesus," she said to a group assembled in the chapel, "before she was born."[21]

Audrey has experienced another inexplicable physical suffering that provides further proof she is a victim soul, according to Linda Santo. During the period when visitors were allowed in the home to view Audrey through her bedroom window, she suddenly came down with a scarlet, hot rash that covered her legs and the lower part of her body. Her pediatrician, Dr. John Harding, had never seen a rash like it and had a biopsy taken to a skin specialist. Dermatologist Dr. Steven Franks recognized Audrey's outbreak as similar to the type experienced by people undergoing chemotherapy treatment. During chemotherapy, the sweat glands may become inflamed and injured, causing a hot rash just like Audrey's to appear. Her legs looked as if they were covered with burns, and her family and caregivers were tormented by not being able to do anything to help her. "We were quite sure that it was very painful to her," said Linda.[22] While studying the biopsy of Audrey's skin, Dr. Franks assumed that it came from a person undergoing chemotherapy. He was very surprised to hear that it wasn't. Eventually the rash disappeared without any medical treatment. Linda stated that this rash occurred in the summer of 1994, when she happened to receive a sudden cluster of calls and letters from people suffering from cancer. Linda described the sudden appearance and disappearance of the rash on Audrey's body coinciding with petitions from the cancer patients as "really incredible. She'd be symptomatic of something that a visitor actually has. Audrey doesn't have it medically but is symptomatic of it."

One of the cancer patients who was cured after visiting Audrey was a woman who had a tumor on her ovary. "Audrey became symptomatic of that," said Linda. (She did not explain how Audrey exhibited this interior tumor in such a way as to prompt the family to have an X ray taken.) "On the X ray," said Linda, "it wasn't a tumor, but a little angel. The doctors were all very excited."[23] According to Linda, the woman's cure is but one recorded in the Santo family's detailed chronicle of healings and miracles attributed to Audrey.

In his book about Audrey, Thomas Petrisko lists two other miraculous healings in which Audrey took another person's suffering upon herself. In one case, a woman called the Santo home from her hospital bed, and the phone was put to Audrey's ear so she could listen to the woman's call for help. The caller was giving birth and having a very difficult delivery. After speaking to Audrey, she felt better and her labor progressed smoothly. Audrey's condition, however, suddenly changed. She began breathing heavily, and her abdomen swelled up. After a few minutes her breathing returned to normal, and her stomach deflated to its original size.[24]

In the next case the visitor was in the Santo's home chapel, standing in line to receive Communion during Mass. This woman, a schoolteacher from New Hampshire, had suffered from multiple sclerosis for many years and was in constant pain. Every step she took was difficult, and as she came closer to the altar, she kept her heart open for a miracle. Suddenly she felt a powerful force within her that caused her to yell out and collapse to the floor. Her pain was completely gone. This event occurred while the Mercy Foundation film crew was taping the Mass for their video, *Audrey's Life*. In that film the teacher said that she felt something strange happening to her in the chapel, and after her collapse she felt better than she had in years. She credits her healing to that Mass and to Audrey. In his book Petrisko adds that when the teacher collapsed, Audrey simultaneously "gasped as if in acute pain from a sudden affliction."[25] This implies that Audrey once again took a person's illness upon herself and provided healing.

From her stigmata to her ability to manifest the symptoms of other people's illnesses, it is believed that Audrey endures suffering in order to be a healing force in the world. Her family and spiritual directors see her suffering as a redemptive, miraculous event and a vital part of God's plan for her. This is one way of trying to make sense of suffering, especially that of a child. Every religion has struggled with the question of why God includes suffering in his creation, and priests and ministers must confront the subject when those in their congregation suffer tragic illness or loss. If God is all-powerful and all-loving, why does he allow people to experience pain, illness, torture? Reverend Audrey Schindler, who trained at Princeton Seminary and is a minister in Melbourne, Australia, has often contemplated the purpose of suffering in her life as well as her ministry. She describes suffering as "a rock on which faith sometimes flounders: 'God's in heaven and all's right with the world' seems to break down when we see a child suffer," she says. "It is a wall we hit our heads against, asking 'why, why, why?' And as long as we ask, and seek, we will find few answers; a few signposts along the way left by those who preceded us in the search, perhaps, but no real, satisfying solution.

"Gradually," Reverend Schindler continues, "another question takes the place of 'why'; that is 'how?' How can we go on in the face of such pain and loss? How can we find those things that make life worth living in spite of what has happened? Theology (especially Western theology) has struggled over the centuries with the problem of theodicy—how can a good God coexist with evil and suffering in the universe? The classical formulation of the dilemma is a triangle. At each of its points: God is good; God is all-powerful; suffering is real. They are nearly impossible to hold in tension. Some views reconcile it all by denying God's power; other views say that God limits God's power, allowing for free will. Another way to reconcile the tension of the theodicy triangle is to say suffering is not really real, it's more a state of mind that one can eventually transcend (as in Buddhism). Or to say that God's goodness might be good in a different way to ours, or to our understanding. This is the 'tapestry' view of suffering. If you look at the back of a piece of needlework, the threads are knotted and tangled, a mess of color and texture. But if you turn it over, a beautiful pattern emerges, one that relies on light and dark for its outline. Such, they say, is the way of human life. On the back, as we see it now, all is at times a tangled mess, cut threads, black lines. But turn it over (in the afterlife or from God's perspective) and the beautiful pattern God intended is clearly seen."

Reverend Schindler does not regard the victim soul concept as justification for suffering. Rather, she sees suffering as a natural part of life that enables us to develop compassion and a closer understanding of one another. "I don't tend to think of our sufferings as having redemptive value," she says. "More, they are part of our participation in the life of all things. All created things suffer at times, and when we feel pain, we are awakened to empathy with others who suffer. Sometimes people say, 'God won't give you more than you can contend with,' referring to suffering. There is a promise in Scripture along these lines, but it refers to temptation, not suffering per se. The lament psalms are one place to find the Jewish response to suffering. There, people pour out their anger and hurt to God and then shift to a *selah,* an interlude and a turning toward hope. It is said that sometimes the more hopeful affirmations at the end of lament psalms were said by the congregation on behalf of the one who was suffering. They kept the faith for them until they could again join in praise."

In *The Varieties of Religious Experience* (1902), William James describes suffering as integral to the life of the worldly hero as well as the religious saint. Humanity has a "common instinct" for revering those who give their lives for others, James maintains. The ascetic life, in which one gives up the world to try to achieve union with God, "symbolizes . . . the belief that there is an element of real wrongness in this world, which is neither to be ignored nor evaded, but which must be squarely met and overcome by an appeal to the soul's heroic resources, and neutralized and cleansed away by suffering."[26] James felt that our deep reverence for this type of self-sacrifice gives "indestructible vital meaning" to the story of Christ's crucifixion, something that is so difficult to grasp with the intellect alone.

Pope John Paul II devoted a chapter to the question of suffering in his book *Crossing the Threshold of Hope*. His response echoes one of the points explored above by Reverend Schindler, in which suffering results because God limits his own power to allow for human free will. "In a certain sense," the pope writes, "one could say that confronted with our human freedom, God decided to make Himself 'impotent.'"[27] Free will enables a human being to inflict pain upon himself or herself or others. But in his omnipotence, explains the pope, God joins people in their suffering as well as their joy. Rather than staying aloof from the ups and downs of humanity, "His wisdom and omnipotence are placed, by free choice, at the service of creation." In this book Pope John Paul II states that God is always in the midst of suffering, whether it is brought about by forces of nature or by humanity. By coming to earth as a man, God endured humankind's suffering and expressed his love in the form of the ultimate sacrifice. "If suffering is present in the history of humanity," he continues, "one understands why His omnipotence was manifested in the omnipotence of humiliation on the Cross." Through suffering, Christ redeemed people's sins and showed God's unending love:

> *God is always on the side of the suffering.* His omnipotence is manifested precisely in the fact He freely accepted suffering. He could have chosen not to do so. He could have chosen to demonstrate His omnipotence even at the moment of the Crucifixion. . . . The fact that He stayed on the Cross until the end, the fact that on the Cross He could say, as do all who suffer: "My God, my God, why have you forsaken me?" (Mark 15:34), has remained in human history *the strongest argument.* If the agony on the Cross had not happened the truth that God is Love would have been unfounded.[28]

Even though God is omnipotent, his love for humanity compels him to give us freedom over our actions. When we choose suffering, says the pope, God is there. "The Man of Suffering is the revelation of that Love which 'endures all things.'" He adds that suffering is also a way for Christians to discover the depth of their faith: "Suffering, in fact, is always a great test not only of physical strength but also of spiritual strength."[29]

Catholic doctrine does not specifically address the concept of victim soul. The Church does, however, describe a sacrament in which people are joined with the Passion of Christ through their personal suffering. The Church catechism states that one of the effects of obtaining the sacrament of the Anointing of the Sick is

> *Union with the passion of Christ.* By the grace of this sacrament the sick person receives the strength and the gift of uniting himself more closely to Christ's Passion: in a certain way he is *consecrated* to bear fruit by configuration to the Savior's redemptive Passion. Suffering, a consequence of original sin, acquires a new meaning; it becomes a participation in the saving work of Jesus.[30]

Through this sacrament, the ill or infirm person is empowered with the Holy Spirit, which gives the strength to endure suffering as well as to heal. The catechism also provides direction about the benefits that can come from suffering an illness. Being sick can lead to despair, but

> it can also make a person more mature, helping him discern in his life what is not essential so that he can turn toward that which is. Very often illness provokes a search for God and a return to him.[31]

Caring for a sick person, or hearing of someone who is facing a debilitating illness with courage, can lead to this fresh perspective, too. Those Christian mystics such as Lydwine of Schiedam who suffered horrible illnesses with cheerful piety had an enormous impact on their visitors, renewing their faith. Many of those who visited Audrey Santo, standing by her bedside or outside the window to her bedroom (before the family stopped these up-close visitations), felt either a new appreciation for their own health or experienced a flash of spiritual awakening or physical healing. Linda Santo believes that one of Audrey's divine missions in life is to help people return to Jesus, echoing the statement in the catechism that an illness can help a person search for God and return to him.

Audrey's physical condition, according to the Santo family and a handful of priests, is sending an important message about life and death to the world. Father Emmanuel McCarthy has spent years studying the messages from various Marian apparition sites throughout the world and connecting them to events in modern history. This study has been part of the work of the priest's Peace and Justice Ministry, an active organization in his parish dedicated to learning and responding to social issues at home and abroad. "The focus of my entire life has been that the Church has to take Jesus' nonviolence more seriously," he said.[32] In his work with apparition messages, Father Emmanuel looks closely for dates that bring the apparitions together with major world events. For example, the last apparition given to Bernadette at Lourdes occurred on July 16, the same date that the first atomic bomb was detonated, eighty-seven years later, in the New Mexico desert. To commemorate this connection, Father Emmanuel inaugurated an annual Mass and prayer vigil at the New Mexico site on July 16. Linda Santo was a member of the group that joined Father Emmanuel in the first twenty-four-hour vigil in July 1990. Looking through Audrey's medical records, Father Emmanuel noticed that the official time of her drowning accident was recorded as 11:03

A.M. on August 9, 1987. He stated that exactly forty-two years earlier, to the exact date and minute, the atomic bomb was dropped on Nagasaki, Japan. (Note: According to numerous sources including the Nagasaki Atomic Bomb Museum, the Smithsonian National Air and Space Museum, and Yale University, the bomb was released at 11:02 A.M.) Addressing a group of people in her chapel, Linda Santo explained that Audrey's accident is linked to the bombing and holds a symbolic meaning. "Eleven-oh-three A.M. on August ninth, 1987, was the accident," she told them. "At 11:03 A.M. the bomb fell on Nagasaki. What people, what human beings destroyed, Audrey is trying to bring back: the sacredness of life."[33]

Father Emmanuel McCarthy views this connection as one more proof that God is trying to save us from nuclear annihilation with miraculous signs like the date of Audrey's accident and messages from Mary at apparition sites. "We have opened a nuclear Pandora's box," he said. "Yet we can still be saved from the consequences of our own evil because God is love, as well as the Lord of history."[34] Father Emmanuel believes that God began showing his concern for potential nuclear war with the Marian apparitions at rue du Bac in Paris in 1930. The nun who received these apparitions was instructed by Mary to create a medal imprinted with the monogram Mary had shown her. She promised the nun that wearers of the medal would receive special protection from the Mother of God. Millions of these medals were eventually made, and the cures, healings, and conversions associated with them were so numerous that the object came to be known as the Miraculous Medal. Father McCarthy believes that with this promise of special protection by Mary, God began giving people an instrument with which to battle the terrible threat of atomic bombs that loomed ahead. "And so," he said, "God, who cares for us and loves us infinitely, began way back . . . in 1930 to take steps through His loving mother, who is the Mother of Humanity, to save us from our own sinfulness."[35]

The Nagasaki bomb, dropped three days after the bombing of Hiroshima, killed approximately seventy thousand instantly and another seventy thousand in the days, years, and decades to follow because of bomb-related causes. Just as Albert Einstein feared, the creation of atomic weapons escalated into an arms race that put the entire world at risk. In 1949 the Soviet Union detonated its first atomic device, followed by the British in 1952. In 1960 France ran its first nuclear test in the Sahara Desert, and in 1964 China exploded its first nuclear bomb. India detonated a bomb below the surface in 1974 and in May of 1998 tested five nuclear devices while Pakistan tested six the same month. Nuclear energy was developed during these decades as well, with meltdown accidents occurring at the Three Mile Island nuclear power plant in Pennsylvania in 1979 and at the Chernobyl nuclear reactor in the Soviet Union in 1986. As nuclear tests continued under and above ground throughout the world, efforts to reduce testing and the proliferation of atomic weapons also undertaken. In 1969 the Strategic Arms Limitation Talks (SALT) between the United States and the Soviet Union began, and after the SALT I treaty expired, a new agreement was signed by those two countries (SALT II). Most recently the Comprehensive Test Ban Treaty

(CTBT) was created in 1996, but it must be ratified by forty-four nations before it can go into effect. As of January 2000, twenty-six nations have ratified the treaty, including Britain, France, Germany, Italy, Japan, Canada, Mexico, and Australia. In October 1999 the U.S. Senate finally voted on the treaty—and voted it down.

The existence of this treaty, however, and other important efforts to tame the world's nuclear arsenals offer the type of hope Father McCarthy describes in his theory about God's intervention in the world. To him and to the Santo family, Audrey is part of the power behind each step forward in the fight against nuclear proliferation. She is also part of the fight against abortion, another issue that Linda believes is central to our "culture of death." By spending time in the Mostar hospital that also served as an abortion clinic in Yugoslavia, Audrey offered herself once again as a symbol of life in a world of death, Linda believes. These events are orchestrated by God, she says, "To show us, like in Scripture, a series of events, to bring us to a culminating point."[36]

Bishop Reilly's ongoing investigation, now in its second phase, is trying to uncover as many medical facts about Audrey as possible before delving into her reported miraculous abilities. How conscious is Audrey? Is she aware enough to have given her consent to become a victim soul at some point since her illness? Does she hear and understand the petitions of her visitors and those who write to her? This is a crucial aspect of the investigation because Audrey's level of awareness will define her ability to voluntarily be of service and, perhaps, to be the recipient of the grace that allows her to be an intercessory between people and God.

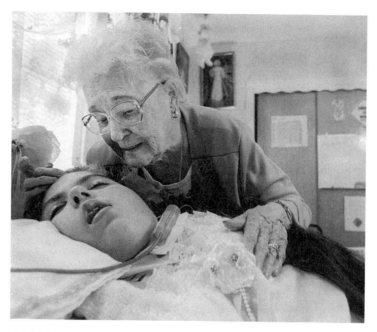

Audrey's grandmother Patricia Nader speaks into Audrey's ear. Before the drowning accident, Audrey was very close to her grandmother and spent much time at her house. (MICHAEL FEIN)

As the investigation continues, inexplicable events show no sign of waning in the Santo home. In addition to taking on the symptoms of other people's illnesses and experiencing the stigmata, Audrey is in the midst of a constant flow of mysterious manifestations in her bedroom and elsewhere in her home. In the presence of Audrey, the images of Christ, Mary, the saints, and the Holy Eucharist are exuding substances that cannot be explained.

5.

Miracles on
Flagg Street

*A miracle cannot prove that which is impossible.
It is useful only as a confirmation of that which
is possible.* —Maimonides

*Every advance of science makes predictable
something that was formerly unpredictable.*
—C. S. Lewis

Some of the conversations Linda had with her husband,
Stephen, while he was incarcerated took the man by surprise.
When Linda told him that oil was showing up on pictures
and statues all over the house, he was skeptical. "When she
started telling me about it, I thought she was crazy," Stephen
recalled. "I said, 'Wow, this woman's lost it.'"[1] When he
came home in 1996, however, he saw the phenomenon for
himself and has lived with it every day. He's as baffled about
where the oil comes from as everyone else.

Visitors to the Santo chapel find themselves surrounded
by a large collection of religious objects, many of which are
covered with an oily sheen. Statues, pictures, and angel
knickknacks are placed on crowded little shelves, on the altar,
and on a table near the back door. They include statues of

Mary as Our Lady of Guadalupe and Our Lady of the Sacred
Heart of Jesus and statues of Jesus as the Infant of Prague
and as the Good Shepherd. Every visitor can see a shiny, oily
film on the head and shoulders of the three-foot-high statue
of Jesus standing on the floor, and the wide streaks of oil cov-
ering a large picture of Mary's face. This picture is placed
over the window, and light coming through the thin paper
makes the streaks even more visible. A faint sweet smell comes
from the oil and permeates the room. On a small statue of
Mary on a shelf near the altar, a cup covers her entire face like
an oversize oxygen mask to collect the oil. A white string
around the head of the large standing Jesus statue holds up a
little cup that catches the drops falling from the tip of his
pointed beard. His left hand is slightly extended, and as I sat
in the pew in front of the statue, I witnessed a drop form on
the index finger in a matter of minutes.

Mary Cormier, a volunteer in her sixties who has devoted
her life to Audrey Santo and her visitors, gave me a mini-tour
of the chapel and talked about the mysterious appearance of
oil and blood on the images. "Everything weeps," she said,
"and some things have wept blood." She pointed out the
faint brown streaks on a bronze crucifix on the altar and explained that blood once flowed on the figure of Jesus. Later,
oil wiped away most of it. A large crucifix on the wall has also
wept blood, she said. This blood, too, has largely been
washed away by oil. The oil flows in streaks down the wall
from the area behind the hands and feet of the Jesus on the
crucifix. Hanging on the back wall is a tapestry reproduction
of Leonardo da Vinci's *The Last Supper* with an oil stain in
the center. With her finger Mrs. Cormier outlined the stain

that takes the shape of a chalice. On the wall next to the picture of Mary is the large, oil-streaked photo of Padre Pio saying Mass with his stigmata clearly visible as a dark, solid patch on his hand. Mrs. Cormier said that oil has appeared on the pages of the missal as well as in the chalice and on the plates that hold the Communion hosts.

Mary Cormier is a soft-spoken, warm, and personable woman. In 1998 she left her home and family in Salem, New Hampshire, to move to Worcester and become the Santo family's spokesperson. She helped form a volunteer organization dedicated to Audrey called the Apostolate of a Silent Soul, which publishes a newsletter and sells videos and other materials about Audrey. "Just coming into the house was an experience I couldn't explain," she said in an article published in *Yankee* magazine in February 2000. "I spent more and more time here," she continued. Her frequent visits became a calling that compelled her to make a big change in her life:

> Pretty soon, I was just here all the time. I've devoted my life to this now. I'm here seven days a week. I miss my kids, I miss the beach. But we formed the Apostolate to help the pilgrims and to help the family. This is an honor. I felt that God called me down here. Audrey has changed my life.[2]

Mrs. Cormier invited everyone in the chapel that day to write down any petitions they might have for Audrey and to drop them in a box at the back of the room. She told us that the notes are read to Audrey every day. Four more people had arrived during my visit, one of whom was a middle-aged woman kneeling behind the pew and praying the rosary. A chant played softly on a boom box, almost blocking out the sound of a television seeping up from the basement. We could also hear people talking inside the house, as normal life goes on in the Santo home on the days that the chapel is open to the public. At one point an electric blender droned from the kitchen and a power tool that sounded like a buzz saw blasted from the backyard.

The family gave the *Washington Post* permission to take a sample of the oil for analysis. "I'd like to know what it is, too," Linda Santo told the newspaper. The sample was sent to Microbac Laboratories in Pittsburgh, which found that it consisted of 80 percent corn or soybean oil and 20 percent chicken fat. The chemist at Microbac, Tom Zierenberg, reported that it is a simple mixture that could be reproduced in any American kitchen. Priests who have witnessed the appearance of oil on the missal and other materials used during Mass sent some samples out for analysis, too. After a pool of oil collected in a chalice in June 1996, the priests sent a sample to the Forensic Analytical lab in Hayward, California. This analysis reported that the substance was olive oil. They sent more samples, taken from the chalice and from one of the statues, to the analytical laboratory of Kraft Food Ingredients in Memphis, Tennessee. There, researcher Boguslaw Lipinski could not precisely identify the oil. He described it as a noncommercial vegetable oil made up of a mixture of the four main fatty acids—palmitic, oleic, linoleic, and linolenic. The oil samples, said Dr. Lipinksi, "did not reveal any characteristic fingerprint for any of the known edible oils. It is certainly a vegetable oil or some natural oil, but we don't know exactly because the fingerprint doesn't fit for anything else."[3]

Results from other tests are also inconclusive. During their filming of a feature on Audrey, the *20/20* production team was given permission to take a sample for analysis, and they reported that the oil was found to be 75 percent olive oil and the rest unidentifiable.

. . .

The first image that wept in the Santo house was a copy of the picture of Our Lady of Guadalupe that had been given to the family as a gift. This famous image represents the Marian apparition seen by an Indian man named Juan Diego in 1531. On his way to Mexico City one day, Diego saw the Virgin Mary on a hilltop. She asked him to go to the local bishop, tell him about the vision, and ask him to build a temple in her honor on the site. When the bishop didn't seem to believe Juan Diego, Mary created a miracle in the form of her own image that appeared on a large cloth Juan Diego wore. This image of Our Lady of Guadalupe has been reproduced for hundreds of years, and the Santo family's was given a prominent place in the living room.

On October 28, 1994, Linda Santo called Father Emmanuel McCarthy with strange yet exciting news. "The image of Our Lady of Guadalupe is dripping oil," she told him. Father McCarthy, who is a former attorney, went to the house with a skeptical attitude. "I was looking for fraud," he said. "People in these difficult situations try to find a tangible evidence of God."[4] He watched the oil stream from the eyes on the picture and couldn't find its source. "I took it apart, I looked at it," he said. "There was no glass on the front, just the canvas on both sides, and I could not see anything that was fraudulent."[5]

Father McCarthy had firsthand experience with miracles. In March 1987 his two-year-old daughter, Benedicta, found a bottle of Tylenol and swallowed a massive overdose. Her liver swelled and became infected, and her doctors at Massachusetts General Hospital diagnosed irreversible liver damage and serious kidney problems. They didn't expect her to survive. Father McCarthy, his wife, and many of their friends prayed to Benedicta's namesake, Sister Teresa Benedicta (Edith Stein) for a healing miracle. The McCarthys had named their daughter after this famous figure because she was born on the anniversary of the nun's death in Auschwitz. Three days after the doctors announced that Benedicta would not survive, she suddenly recovered—her liver and kidneys were perfectly healthy. Dr. Ronald Klein man could find no organic reason for the recovery, calling it a miracle: "I think you have to acknowledge that there are other forces in play beyond what we're capable of doing."[6] After the miracle was reported to the Vatican, the pope summoned Dr. Kleinman to Rome to testify about Benedicta's recovery. On April 8, 1987, Pope John Paul II declared the miracle authentic, which paved the way for the canonization of Edith Stein. She was declared a saint on October 11, 1998.

Reports of weeping images like the one Father McCarthy examined in the Santo home have increased in modern times. Highly publicized recent sites of this phenomenon include Civitavecchia, near Rome, where a statue of Mary brought from Medjugorje began weeping in its garden shrine in 1995. It weeps tears of blood, and DNA testing by the Catholic Church confirms that the blood is human. Statues wept tears in the presence of Father James Bruse of Virginia, the priest who has also suffered the stigmata. In the early 1990s he noticed that after he touched statues, those in his office as well as in the sanctuary, they began to weep. When he celebrated Mass at a nearby church, a wooden statue of the Virgin Mary there also began to weep tears. In Rooty Hill, a town near Sydney, Australia, a statue of Our Lady of Fátima began weeping in 1994. A sixteen-year-old boy bought the statue at an antique shop, and when news spread about the drops of liquid rolling down the statue's face, dozens of people visited the home every day. Also in 1994 a statue of Mary began weeping blood in the home of a retired postal worker in County Wicklow, Ireland. So many people flocked to her home that she finally had the statue moved to a public place in the village. In 1997 a statue in a convent of Franciscan nuns in Benin, Africa, began weeping tears of blood. In Las Vegas a statue of Our Lady of Guadalupe brought from the basilica in Mexico City began weeping tears in the Covarrubias family's backyard shrine in 1998. The tears are collected in cotton balls and given to visitors, just as the oil is collected from the Santos' statues and given to those who request it. In 1992 a six-inch-high porcelain statue of the Virgin Mary owned by a housewife in Chile began weeping tears that appeared to be blood. The liquid was tested and confirmed to be human. These are but a few of the many contemporary reports of miracles surrounding statues of the Virgin Mary and other religious figures.

Unlike the above examples, the liquid that flows from the statues and images in the Santo home is oil, only seldom blood. Oil has always played an important role in the rituals of Christianity, which views it as a symbol of the Holy Spirit. The Catholic catechism explains that "the symbolism of anointing with oil also signifies the Holy Spirit, to the point of becoming a synonym for the Holy Spirit. . . . Christ (in Hebrew 'messiah') means the one 'anointed' by God's Spirit."[7] In *The Rites of Christian Initiation*, Maxwell E. Johnson states that rituals of conversion/baptism in the early Church portrayed putting off the old nature and being clothed with the new nature of Christ and may have included oil as well as water. "Anointings with oil," he writes, "develop in all early Christian liturgical traditions to express ritually the gift, anointing, and seal of the Holy Spirit in initiation."[8] In the New Testament Jesus is described as the one who baptizes with the Holy Spirit, unlike John the Baptist, who baptizes with water. According to Maxwell Johnson, because oil symbolizes the Holy Spirit, it was an important part of the ritual in the first centuries—perhaps even more important than water. The Holy Spirit represented by the oil also had the power to protect Christians, as described in this excerpt from a fourth-century baptism service:

This power the oil of anointing imparts: not the oil, but the Spirit that gives it power. The Spirit gives

power to the unction of the feeble oil. . . . By its firm-
ness it makes firm the body and the faculties of the
soul, and they go forth confidently to wage war against
the Evil One. . . . The Name of the Divinity looks out
from the sign on the forehead: and the eyes of the
crafty one are ashamed to look on it.[9]

In fifth-century Rome oil was used in Christian rituals to
anoint and bless parts of the body. Johnson writes that the
nostrils were anointed so that they would "be led to [the
Savior's] spiritual odor by a certain inexpressible sweetness."
The ears were touched with holy oil "because faith enters the
mind," and with anointing the ears would be "protected by
a kind of holy wall."[10]

In the Catholic Church, a mixture of olive oil and balsam
is blessed by a bishop to become *chrism,* a consecrated mixture for use in baptism, confirmation, the blessing of objects,
and other rites. Used in a prebaptismal anointing ritual, oil
symbolizes cleansing; used for anointing the sick, it represents soothing and healing; used in the confirmation ritual, it
gives the Christian the seal of the Holy Spirit forever.

Soon after oil started flowing from the picture of Our
Lady of Guadalupe in Audrey Santo's home in 1994, the
phenomenon spread to other objects in the house. The chalice next to the tabernacle in Audrey's room fills with oil.
(The family received permission from the bishop to keep a
consecrated Communion host, housed in a special recepta-
cle, in the house.) Father Leroy Smith, director of Our Lady
of the Holy Spirit Center in Cincinnati, Ohio, led a pilgrimage to the Santo home in October 1997. While celebrating

Mass there, he witnessed oil appearing on many objects. "The containers on the altar," he told a group in Cincinnati after returning from Worcester, "before we ever began Mass, were filling up with oil." He described this most remarkable Mass as follows:

The large host the priest uses at the Mass was almost soaked with oil by the time mass began. The chalice wherein the precious blood would be present was oozing oil all inside of it and gathering at the bottom. Not only that, the suborium, in which the hosts were to be placed, was also filling up with oil right before our eyes, I mean you could stand there and watch it. This is something that has to be supernatural, miraculous. When it came time to give out communion, I gave out the hosts at this Mass, and I had trouble getting the hosts separated one from the other because they were so saturated with this holy oil, this miraculous oil. And of course when the people received this precious blood, it also was full of this holy oil, this miraculous oil. At the point in the mass when little Audrey goes to communion, Linda, the mother, is given a host and it's placed in a little container and she takes it in and gives the host to little Audrey. Before she gave the host to Audrey she said that she noticed some kind of fluid coming out of the little host. And pretty soon it filled the bottom of this little container, and actually the host was swimming almost in this liquid. She gave the host to Audrey and she brought it back so we could see what had happened. This had never, ever happened before. And the aroma from that liquid, it wasn't like the oil on the other things, it was completely different, very fluid, and a beautiful aroma from that liquid. We told Linda that she should go out and let everyone that was there have an opportunity not only to see it, but to experience the odor from that liquid. After she brought it back in, she said, "Father, what do you think that is?" And off of the top of my head, I don't even know where this came from, I said, "Well, Linda, I think those are the tears of Christ coming out of the Eucharist. Not tears of sadness or sorrow, but tears of happiness and joy."[11]

Earlier that year Father Smith had participated in another Mass at the Santo home in which a crucifix on the altar suddenly began to bleed. He saw blood flowing from the side of the figure of Jesus, but because the Mass had begun, he couldn't say anything. He simply pointed to the blood so the congregation would look at it and continued celebrating the Mass. "Of course, all the people there were staring in amazement," he said. "It wasn't five minutes later that the whole chest of Christ on the crucifix was covered in blood." He wondered why this was happening and thought that perhaps "Christ was trying to show us in a very special way that we were on Calvary with Christ at the Holy Sacrifice of the Mass."[12]

There are two tabernacles in Audrey's room: one for holding the Communion host that Linda breaks into tiny pieces and feeds her every day (pieces small enough to melt on her tongue) and one for containing four bloodstained

Communion hosts. Visitors can see one of these mysterious bloody hosts in the chapel, and all are brought out for public display on each annual Anniversary Day.

Blood first appeared on a Communion host in Audrey's room in 1995. One day the priests opened the tabernacle to find a dark stain on the host and a smear of wet, fresh liquid on the surface of the container. The liquid was tested and found to be blood. The following year, during a Mass in the chapel that was being filmed by the Mercy Foundation, blood suddenly appeared on one of the hosts. During the Mass the priest uses one large host as well as smaller hosts that are placed on a small plate. On June 5, 1996, Father George Joyce of Springfield, Massachusetts, Father Tom McCarthy of Chicago, and Father Leo Potvin of Newport, New York, were celebrating Mass. Father Joyce held up the large host, saying, "Take this, all of you, and eat it; this is my body which will be given up for you." When he lowered the host to the tray, the smaller host had a large splotch of blood on it. He paused, then slid the tray toward the congregation and tilted it so they could see the host. Gasps broke out through the small group, and he motioned them to be quiet so the Mass could continue.

When Mass was over, the Mercy Foundation producers talked to the priests and the visitors about this supernatural event. "I was flabbergasted," said Father McCarthy. "I didn't know what to say, what to do. I knew a miracle was taking place. . . . It was a miraculous event, and I was privileged to witness that." There were two priests from India in the chapel that day who had been drawn by stories of miracles in the Santo home. The unexpected appearance of blood on the host renewed their faith. "After seeing this personally," said Father Bala Bachimala, "my faith has grown. I am touched."[13]

According to Roman Catholic doctrine, Christ becomes present at the Mass during the *transubstantiation*, the moment when the bread and wine transform into his actual body and blood. This true body and blood is called the *Eucharist*, which has only the appearance of bread and wine. Pope John Paul II has written about the Eucharist as the central part of the mystery of faith, and the Mass (the sacrament of the Eucharist) as an event that affects all people and all creation:

> The priesthood, in its deepest reality, is *the priesthood of Christ*. It is Christ who offers himself, his Body and Blood, in sacrifice to God the Father, and by this sacrifice makes righteous in the father's eyes all mankind and, indirectly, all creation. The priest, in his daily celebration of the Eucharist, goes to the very heart of this mystery. For this reason the celebration of the Eucharist must be the most important moment in the priest's day, the center of his life.[14]

Supernatural phenomena involving Communion hosts that have been officially recognized as miracles by the Catholic Church are known as Eucharistic miracles. Some Eucharistic miracles involve the production of flesh in addition to the appearance of human blood. The first such miracle in the history of the Catholic Church was of this type. In the eighth century a monk at the Church of St. Legontian in what is now Lanciano, Italy, was struggling with the idea of Christ's actual presence in the Eucharist. As the doubting priest celebrated Mass one day, the host he was holding suddenly turned into flesh and the wine in the goblet turned into clotted blood. Through the centuries these objects have retained their shape and have been kept in a silver reliquary in the church. Scientists made an analysis in 1981 and discovered that the flesh is human heart tissue and that the blood is human. Both the flesh and the blood have the blood type AB. The scientists were impressed that the tissue and blood had remained so well preserved after twelve centuries. This Eucharistic miracle is on display in the cathedral at Lanciato, a town near the eastern coast of Italy, about a hundred miles east of Rome.

This type of miracle recently occurred in Korea. Julia Kim (the stigmatist discussed previously) was attending an outdoor Mass in the mountains near the town of Naju on September 22, 1995, when the host on her tongue reportedly changed into flesh and blood. Bishop Roman Danylak, who celebrated the Mass with two priests, testified in a signed statement that he witnessed the Eucharistic miracle. "Father Joseph Finn," wrote the bishop, "saw the white edge of the host disappearing and changing into the substance of living flesh. Father Chang and I returned to Julia. The host had changed to dark red, living flesh and blood flowing from it."[15] After Mass Julia Kim told the priests that the flesh moved and grew larger in her mouth, making it difficult to swallow. This was not the first time the Communion host had reportedly transformed for Mrs. Kim, nor would it be the last. On October 31, 1995, she visited the Vatican with her husband, her daughter, and a priest from Korea. Her Eucharistic miracles were known to the pope, and the group was invited to attend a private Mass celebrated by him. During this Mass, in view of Pope John Paul II and the other priests present, the host on Mrs. Kim's tongue turned into a fleshy object the shape of a heart.

Another miracle that received bishop's approval in the 1990s took place in Betania, Venezuela. On December 8, 1991, blood appeared on one part of a Communion host that had been broken into four pieces by the priest. A sample of the blood was tested and found to be human. Manifestation of blood on a Communion host was reported by a priest and his congregation in Barbeau, Michigan, in 1996, but the local bishop did not investigate. The same type of miracle occurred at a Mass in Marlboro, New Jersey, in 1994, but the local bishop also chose not to investigate the case.

The events on South Flagg Street *are* under official investigation, however, and priests from all over the world visit the Santo home to observe the four hosts stained with human blood that are kept in Audrey's room. The lives of priests, as stated by the pope, revolve around the mystery of the Eucharist, and many of them have drawn inspiration from their visits. Father Emmanuel McCarthy claims that in the Santo home "Jesus has exposed the reality of what he does in the Mass. Audrey, at three years old, was called on by our Lord to turn her life over, to surrender her life, and she did. She did! . . . God has poured out his proofs! Four hosts have bled; the proof is overwhelming."[16]

Those who visit the Santo family chapel and witness the oil and the bloodstained host come to see something that can't be explained, to feel a peaceful presence, to pass on their prayer requests to Audrey Santo, to get healed, or simply to satisfy their curiosity.

The *48 Hours* program on Audrey featured a woman with cancer who visited the Santo home and claimed that it gave her healing. Andrea Pearson had fought breast cancer for five years and had recently learned that the disease had spread to her liver and bones. The mother of three young children, she was praying for a miracle and hoped to find one in Audrey. She went to the Santo home with a friend and was invited to view Audrey through the window in her bedroom wall. "We got to look at her through the glass," she said. "She's gorgeous. I mean, she's absolutely beautiful. She just had sort of this very peacefulness about her." Two weeks after her visit, Mrs. Pearson had another CAT scan and was stunned to learn that "there was no sign of any cancer, nothing. . . . My liver was completely clear." Her oncologist attributed her improvement to a drug treatment that had already started to show results before the visit to Audrey. "I know there are medical explanations," Andrea said, "but in my heart, I know I got a miracle." Months later, however, she was hit with bad news once again. The cancer had moved to her brain. This did not dampen her belief in Audrey's miracle, because she believed Audrey had already given her more time with her family. "I truly believe God has given her some sort of gift," she said, "and I think she shared that with me. How long will I be here for my children? I don't know. But for every day that I am here, I thank God and I truly believe God is the one that's made the difference."[17]

Even though people can no longer view Audrey in her

home, hundreds have written to Linda Santo to tell her that they have been healed by visiting the chapel. Linda has set up a file for letters and claims of healing. Something happens to them when they see the oil flowing and hear Linda or volunteers tell them stories about Audrey's miraculous survival in Medjugorje and the special relationship she has with Jesus. Not everyone who visits the chapel experiences miracles or spiritual epiphanies, of course. There are people who are not moved by the sheen on the statues, the stains on the walls, and the idea that Audrey is a victim soul. This is not necessarily a negative experience, because some come away with a renewed conviction that they don't need outward signs to feel secure in their beliefs. To these visitors, the weeping icons and "personality cult" that has grown around Audrey Santo appear to be the result of superstitious rather than deeply religious people.

Sam T., a graphic designer from Connecticut, visited the chapel because he had had an inspirational experience at Lourdes. He had seen the story about Audrey Santo on *48 Hours* and "was curious to see if the same kind of aura of peace and devotion existed in the Santo garage," he explained. "It was Lourdes on a much, much smaller scale in many respects. There was definitely a special feeling in the chapel; the devotion of the other people in the room set up an atmosphere of peace and love that could be interpreted as Audrey's blessing on the place. Whatever the source, it was real and palpable. I was raised Catholic, so I suppose I'm predisposed to believe stuff I haven't got a clue about. It makes sense to me that people are praying to Audrey without knowing what is going on. I do think it's all a matter of interpretation. In the end, if it brings love to the surface, it's a good thing." Sam didn't find any inspiration in the oil-covered statues, even though he'd never seen anything like it before. "I guess I've seen too many TV shows debunking this kind of thing to believe totally, much as I'd like to," he said. "There seem to be so many possible explanations. It could all very well come from God, but weeping oil, bleeding hosts, and stigmata don't say a lot for God's imagination."

On the subject of Audrey's ability to heal people and bring their prayers to God, Sam feels that "anything, of course, is possible, but my sense of God is more personal. I think we all carry God within us, and the idea that someone else can intercede is ludicrous. Audrey may have an especially strong sense of God within herself, but I doubt that the healing of other people comes from her. I think we can heal ourselves with faith. Maybe Audrey is just a mirror off of which we can bounce that faith back into ourselves. That's not such a bad thing to be."

Cynthia T. was another visitor who left the chapel without having been overly impressed by the statues and stories. She grew up in a religious family in Texas and had always been fascinated by the many ways people expressed their faith. Even though she was brought up with religion, she never found the deep mystery that, as a child, she thought would be found in the Church. "I grew up in a very religious family," she said. "My father was a preacher, and life was a pilgrimage. Even as a child, I watched and listened intently, hoping to see something spectacular (actually, I would have settled for mildly interesting). I never did, and I was always disappointed. In my opinion, there was nothing in the Audrey chapel that couldn't easily be reproduced in anyone's garage. I put my glasses on and watched one of the statues patiently, hoping for even one tiny drip. I saw nothing except what was there when I arrived—oily-looking statues with partially filled cups hanging from their heads. The woman at the chapel told me that Audrey's eyes sometimes dart around, as if this is evidence of something holy. Maybe she's trying to tell somebody of her pain. I'm afraid that after my visit and hearing the woman talk about Audrey's 'mission' as a 'victim soul,' I'm convinced that she's an unfortunate child who is being badly exploited."

Skeptics, clergy, seekers, believers—people of many viewpoints visit the Santo home and come away inspired, renewed, healed, skeptical, confused, or even, in the case of Cynthia, angry. Mary Cormier is never ruffled by visitors who don't appear to be spiritually enriched by their chapel visit. "Audrey has given peace and hope to so many," she said, "but you are always going to find people who are skeptical. The fact that Audrey is still living, after all she has been through, is a miracle in itself."[18]

The question of why the supernatural events in the Santo home are happening is as interesting as the question of how they are produced. Bleeding Communion hosts, physical healing, weeping and moving statues, stigmata—Audrey's life is a virtual encyclopedia of mystical phenomena. Why are these things occurring in her home, and why is there such an increase in Marian apparitions and miraculous claims throughout the world? Linda Santo states that Audrey is bringing people to Jesus, "back to the sacraments, and she's a statement of life in our culture of death."[19] To Linda and many others close to her, Audrey is a testament that God considers every life—even the severely disabled and the unborn—precious. Father Emmanuel McCarthy believes that the date and time of Audrey's accident links her to the bombing of Nagasaki and creates a message that life always triumphs, even in the nuclear age. Father Leroy Smith believes that Audrey is bringing people closer to the real meaning of the Eucharist. "Christ doesn't work miracles for no reason," he said. "I think, through little Audrey and her sufferings and through these miracles that are happening, that souls, more souls and more souls, will be brought back to Christ. . . . Something like this that is happening in the world will hopefully bring people to an understanding of Christ's true and real presence in the Eucharist."[20]

Father James Bruse believes that God made the Lake Ridge statues weep and gave him the stigmata so that people would be motivated to return to God. "I explain it all as Christ saying He wants His people to come back," he said. "He is saying that Mary is there to intercede. It has been her image and her statues that have been changing color and weeping. I think she plays a part in it."[21] Many of the messages brought to the Marian visionaries around the world are calls to return to prayer, to a spiritual discipline, and to a life in which God is at the center.

In recent years spiritual messages from mysterious sources have reached millions of people through books such as *A Course in Miracles* and Neale Donald Walsch's *Conversations with God* series. And for thousands of people who have visited Audrey Santo or her chapel, personal messages have come through mysterious signs and manifestations. For two

Visitors to the Santo home looking through a window that was cut into the wall in Audrey's bedroom. The family stopped these visits after the local bishop voiced his concern about the number of people moving through the house and potentially disrupting the family's ability to care for Audrey. (MICHAEL FEIN)

thousand years the strange and extraordinary lives of mystics have unveiled aspects of spirituality that dogma doesn't touch. Unusual examples of religious experience continue to flourish in the twenty-first century around the world and, in the Tatnuck neighborhood of Worcester, across the street.

"The mystical needs of human beings are so urgent," wrote Geoffrey Parrinder, "that they will seek their satisfaction wherever it may be found. Or, in a more theological interpretation, the divine Spirit is seeking man, and will not be restricted to forms or theories."[22]

6.

Miracles or
Mind Power?

Miracles do not happen in contradiction of nature, but in contradiction of what we know about nature.   —Saint Augustine (354–430)

I shall not commit the fashionable stupidity of regarding everything I cannot explain as a fraud.   —C. G. Jung (1875–1961)

The New Testament contains dozens of stories about miracles performed by Jesus before and after his death, such as raising a man from the dead, restoring a severed ear, healing a blind man, and freeing an apostle from prison. Christianity, both Catholic and Protestant, revolves around sacraments that contain miraculous elements: baptism frees people from original sin, for example, and Holy Communion/Eucharist binds the family of believers with Jesus. The miraculous aspect of these sacraments makes Christianity a *salvific* religion, in which salvation from sin comes about through sacred rituals. Miracles also play a role in defining the holiest of the Catholic faithful, the saints. One of the conditions of sainthood is proof that miracles occurred through his or her intercession.

Miracles have a different significance in Judaism, where they are divided into "hidden" and "revealing" miracles. A revealing miracle is an extraordinary event that runs counter to the laws of nature, such as parting the Red Sea in the Old Testament. Rather than dwelling on these rare supernatural events, however, Judaism places much more emphasis on hidden miracles, wondrous occurrences that are so much a part of ordinary life that they are often overlooked. Hidden miracles include the air we breathe, the body's ability to heal, and the beauty of nature. Both types of miracles share a common element: they are performed by an omnipotent God who created everything. Therefore, there is no difference between the natural and the supernatural, because everything is part of God's world.

As discussed previously, the supernatural events occurring around Audrey Santo have been interpreted by the family and many priests as miracles with religious meaning. Devout Catholics, the Santos perceive the weeping statues, blood-stained Communion hosts, and stigmata as signs from God. "It's God working with Audrey as an instrument," said Linda. "God takes such good care of her. She's like a beautiful, perfect icon."[1] Linda Santo's files are filled with hundreds of letters from people who also believe God worked through Audrey to heal them.

Bishop Reilly set up his investigation to determine whether these events are of divine origin. In summarizing the ambiguous results of the first phase of the inquiry, Dr. John Madonna, a psychotherapist, admitted that it may never be possible to explain the events as either natural or divine. "In the final analysis," he said, "it may simply be a matter of faith."[2]

The interpretation of miraculousness given by the Santo family and others is a matter of faith, but there are other perspectives from which to view such phenomena. Audrey Santo's supernatural mysteries can be explored in terms of the mind-body connection, hypnotism, and other medical models. The stigmata and other physical manifestations can be discussed in the realm of transpersonal and depth psychology, which deal with the invisible psyche as a source of events in the visible world. They can also be viewed through the lens of parapsychology and psychokinesis, the ability of the mind to act upon objects in the environment.

Could Audrey Santo's stigmata be an example of the mind's ability to affect the body? In the field of medicine, the past four decades have brought discoveries about the connection between the mind and the body. Just as the concept of miracles erases the line between natural and supernatural, science is taking away the line between the "formless" mind and the physical body. Mood and attitude—invisible and nonmaterial—are now considered directly related to the integrity of the immune system. This relationship has come to light thanks to a new branch of medicine called psychoneuroimmunology, which deals with the chemical effects of emotions on the body. The patient's anxiety over an illness, trust in the doctor, faith in the treatment—each of these emotional elements has been found to have a bearing on how the body heals. A pioneer in this research, Candace Pert, describes how the material world of brain chemicals affects the nonmaterial world of the mind/emotions in her book *Molecules of Emotion* (1997). This research led to the discovery that therapies such as relaxation techniques and guided imagery can have a positive effect on fighting disease. What was previously considered "just" mind, in terms of how the physical body works, is now known to have a vital impact on the body at the cellular level.

Experiments have been conducted in which a cancer patient mentally visualizes his or her immune system attacking the disease, which results in more killer cell activity (T cells that attack toxins and bacteria). Larry Dossey, M.D., points out that the relationship between mind and matter, which is the basis of a revolution in medicine, is similar to the relationship between energy and matter discovered by Einstein:

> As with energy and matter, mind and matter may be equivalent even though they appear completely different. And just as energy and matter are related through a third entity, the speed of light [E=mc²], mind and matter also may be related through a third entity, *meaning*. . . . We know a lot about "positive biology"—physiological changes associated with hope, love, and optimism. Consequently we may believe we understand how meaning enters the body and actually changes it.[3]

A theory about the cause of the stigmata, which Linda Santo claims has happened to Audrey more than fifty times, can be put forth based on the mind-body connection. Studies with hypnosis have shown that the mind affects physical changes in the body. About 70 percent of people are able to go into a hypnotic trance on some level, and a very small percentage—4 percent—are considered highly hypnotizable. Under hypnosis, the subject can translate a mental image into a bodily change. The skin is particularly sensitive to thoughts and feelings—we blush when we're embarrassed and flush red when we're angry. Therefore, hypnosis works well in treating skin problems such as psoriasis and burns. Dr. Dabney Ewin, a physician and hypnotist in New Orleans, has been treating burns hypnotically for more than thirty years. In 1978 he had a case in which a man fell into 950-degree molten lead up to his knees. Dr. Ewin was able to see the worker immediately after the accident and used hypnosis to suggest coolness and healing. This type of injury would normally create third-degree burns that would require skin grafts and a long hospitalization, but with hypnosis treatment the patient had only second-degree burns and didn't have to undergo any painful skin grafting.

In many of the cases that have been recorded, the stigmata usually begin as pain and redness of the skin and develop into an open wound. They have also appeared as blood on the surface, without any broken skin. In the 1930s a doctor experimented with hypnosis to create the stigmata on a patient's body. In *The Bleeding Mind,* Ian Wilson describes these experiments, which took place when the stigmatic Therese Neumann was headline news in Europe. Dr. Alfred Lechler had been working with a twenty-six-year-old woman, Elizabeth, who, after recovering from influenza, suffered from partial paralysis, headaches, double vision, and other serious problems. However, she had progressed well by Good Friday in 1932, the day she attended a talk about the crucifixion. During the talk the speaker showed slides with illustrations of the crucifixion process, and as she watched, Elizabeth felt pain in her hands and feet in the same spots where the nails were driven into the victim in the slides. When she told Dr. Lechler about her pain and when it started, he got the idea that perhaps Therese Neumann's stigmata was inflicted the same way—by a powerful suggestion.

To test his theory, Dr. Lechler (whose ethics in this case are questionable) induced hypnosis and asked Elizabeth to concentrate on the idea of real nails being driven into her hands and feet. As usual, when she came out of the trance, she didn't remember anything that had been suggested to her. The next morning she had bleeding wounds on her hands and feet and was terrified that she was turning into another Therese Neumann. Elizabeth had seen gruesome photographs in the newspaper of Neumann with wide, dark streaks of blood streaming down her face. The doctor consoled her by saying that she would be able to make the wounds disappear as easily as she made them appear. In the meantime, he asked her to cooperate in another experiment. Without using hypnosis, he asked Elizabeth to concentrate on the bloody tears of Therese Neumann and imagine that her eyes were bleeding in the exact same way. She focused on this thought while doing some housework in the afternoon, and to Dr. Lechler's amazement she returned to him with blood pouring down her cheeks. He immediately gave her the suggestion that the bleeding stop, and it did. The doctor repeated these experiments several times and got the same results. He and a nurse were always present to make sure Elizabeth wasn't self-inflicting the wounds. Author Ian Wilson concluded:

> The significance of all this is profound. Effectively Lechler can be said to have established more authoritatively than anyone before or since that spontaneous

bleedings of the type attributed to stigmatics during the last seven centuries really do happen, and that these can be demonstrated under properly controlled conditions . . . [and] . . . that the stigmatic, even without having been formally hypnotized, seems to be, during his or her bleedings, in a mental and physical state effectively indistinguishable from hypnosis.[4]

Photographs of Audrey Santo's stigmata have not been released, but Linda has described them as bleeding that comes from her hands, feet, head, side, and even her tracheostomy and feeding tubes. A comment by Ray Delisle, spokesman for the Worcester diocese, offers a hint that the bleeding is slight. "We're not necessarily talking about a case where you have a profusion of blood from the wounds," he said in the local press.[5] Speculating with the hypnosis theory of the stigmata, Audrey would be manifesting Christ's wounds as the result of a suggestion or her own mental focus on the Passion. This is shaky ground, because her brain damage, as stated by Dr. Kaye, is extensive. If Audrey doesn't have the ability to focus on something, where then would the mental process of hypnosis come from? If not a result of her own thoughts, could Audrey's manifestation of the stigmata be the result of someone else's concentration on the Passion (such as a close family member), mysteriously being projected onto her?

A psychiatrist presented with a patient who was bleeding from the palms and feet for no apparent reason would try to rule out many things before considering that the patient was obsessed with the wounds of Christ. "Psychiatrists," said Dr.

Marc Feldman of Birmingham, Alabama, "being physicians and immersed in the scientific technique as part of their training, definitely would look askance at that type of claim. We would consider fifty or sixty other possibilities as a higher priority, and only the most spiritual among us would be willing to entertain the notion that this is authentic. The question is: if it is not as the individual has reported it, not spontaneous stigmata as a source of deep religious belief, what is it?"

Dr. Feldman, whose psychiatric practice specializes in factitious (exaggerated or self-induced) illness, has seen the mind-body connection at work. "It is utterly remarkable how influential people's attitudes, thoughts, beliefs and feelings can affect them physically," he said, "even in ways that doctors and others might have viewed impossible. Yet, in my work, and this is true of other physicians, we are confronted at times with no explanation other than that some kind of mental state caused the physical concern for which the patient is presenting. The problem sometimes arises that we do three million dollars' worth of tests before we consider the influence of mind on the body—the rich interplay of the chemical messengers in the brain and the influence of brain neurons on the body. There have been more scientific studies done on things that looked really 'soft' to a doctor in the past, such as meditation, and which are now looking more scientifically viable."

In medicine, the mind-body connection is held responsible for a perplexing type of wound called psychogenic purpura (bruising or lesions originating in the mind), or when no physical explanation can be given for the wounds and

134

spontaneous bleeding. Like a stigmatic, a person who suffers from psychogenic purpura manifests wounds or bleeding after thinking about a trauma, but in this case an event the patient experienced. In rare cases, however, the psychogenic purpura has manifested after the patient thought about someone else's trauma. In *Stigmata: A Medieval Mystery in a Modern Age,* author Ted Harrison describes a case of psychogenic purpura in which a woman manifested bruises and bleeding on her leg after going through an emotional recollection of the day she saw her neighbor get shot in the thigh.

The psychological profiles of people who suffer from psychogenic purpura contain experiences that parallel those of stigmatics: hallucinations (visions), the ability to endure pain beyond normal limits (joyful suffering of the wounds of Christ), and emotional concentration on past injuries (devotional focus on the Passion). "Drawing parallels between psychogenic purpura and stigmata," writes Harrison, "suggests that a similar psychosomatic mechanism is involved in producing both sets of marks."[6]

Another realm of science, parapsychology, describes a phenomenon that has intriguing similarities to the events surrounding Audrey Santo. The term *poltergeist* usually conjures up an image of vases flying across the room in a house where an adolescent is going through the hormonal ups and downs of puberty. The phenomena are sometimes attributed to a ghost or spirit, but parapsychologists also theorize that the activities may be the work of a mass of energy formed during a dramatic trauma surrounding the young person. This chaotic mass of energy is under the unconscious control of this individual and ignites a variety of events. Psychokinesis, the power of the mind to move, alter, or otherwise affect inanimate objects, is sometimes considered responsible for poltergeist phenomena. A number of characteristics related to poltergeist activity correspond to events in Audrey's life, as shown in the following list:

Poltergeist characteristic	Audrey Santo event
Trauma in the personal history	Audrey drowned and was revived
Odd odors and smells	Visitors claim to smell roses and/or other pleasant scents in Audrey's room and chapel
Breezes in closed areas	In the Medjugorje apparition room, Linda Santo saw Audrey's hair moving as if from a slight breeze, although there were no open windows or fans
Moving objects	Nurses and family members claim that the statues in Audrey's room shift position on their own to face the tabernacle that holds the Communion host
Blood on walls, floors, ceilings	Blood has appeared on statues, pictures, Communion hosts, and other objects used in the Mass; a pool of blood was found on the inside of the tabernacle on Good Friday in 1996

Reports of poltergeists sometimes describe frightening and even violent outbursts of energy, which is not the case in the Santo home. An argument could be made that the same psychokinetic activities are responsible for the phenomena, but in Audrey's case they are being filtered through a household environment filled with strong religious overtones. Instead of blood showing up on a wall, it manifests on a religious statue and a consecrated Communion wafer. Rather than disturbing, unpleasant odors, the energy manifests as the sweet, roselike scent associated with apparitions of the Virgin Mary.

Poltergeist phenomena may be an awkward, out-of-control attempt on the part of our deepest self to get a message through, according to the renowned psychoanalyst Marie-Louise von Franz. A Jungian analyst and author, von Franz (1915–98) worked closely with Carl Jung for nearly thirty years until his death in 1961. In her book *Psyche and Matter*, von Franz discusses the Self, the guiding principle within us that has a far broader perspective than the ego or conscious mind. According to analytical psychology, this inner guide orchestrates our dreams in an attempt to help us understand more about life than we can perceive in ordinary, day-to-day reality. The Self gives us access to the world of archetypes and divine experiences, and expresses itself in various ways. If these messages are ignored, the Self keeps trying in ways that may be misleading, such as poltergeist phenomena. "Apparently the positive aspect of the Self," she writes, "can only manifest when the individual ego concentrates upon the Self and tries to realize its messages creatively." If it does not do so, she continues, the same unconscious contents show their tendency toward self-manifestation in poltergeist phenomena and meaningless spooky events. The latter have no meaning, but perhaps could have a meaning if only the ego would look for it. . . . This is a problem which modern parapsychology should investigate.[7]

Analytical psychology approaches the mind-matter connection in terms of synchronicity, a term coined by C. G. Jung. Synchronicity is the meaningful coincidence of outer and inner events, such as a clock that stops at the exact time of a person's death. These peculiar connections reveal a link between the mind and the physical world, and the concept of synchronicity can be applied to weeping religious statues and icons. The mystic's focus on the Passion is the inner event that manifests itself as an outer event—blood on a statue of Jesus. The blood doesn't appear on a doorknob or a coffee cup; it shows up on an object that precisely corresponds to the mystic's thoughts. Synchronistic events usually occur during crucial phases of personal development, signaling that a new level of awareness is about to break through.

Dr. Thayer Greene, a Jungian analyst and Protestant minister from Massachusetts, has a view on how synchronicity may be occurring in Audrey's life. "One way of possibly understanding these phenomena is that Audrey has no way of experientially, individually communicating with any level of consciousness," he said. "Synchronistically, the only way that energy can be expressed is through the weeping objects. It's not inappropriate to use the word 'weeping' because her situation is one of such terrible tragedy and sadness."

Dr. Greene also commented that Linda Santo's lifelong devotion to her religion and her childhood desire to become a nun may play a role in the family's ideas about Audrey's holiness and divine mission. "Perhaps the saint that Linda could not be, because she did not fulfill her own desire to become a nun, is the saint her daughter must be," he said. "Audrey is the ultimate blank screen upon which everyone can project their own psyche and their own longing." Also, this preoccupation with saintliness may give rise to a negative element in the family system that tries to compensate for it. "Wherever you find a saint, you're going to find a 'demon,' a negative energy," said Dr. Greene. "You're going to find a dark side to go with that saintliness." Many stories describe the demons that mystics and stigmatics like Padre Pio and Teresa of Ávila battled publicly and privately. People close to the altar when Padre Pio celebrated Mass saw him swat at invisible figures and overheard him commanding them to go away. The more powerful Padre Pio's connection to God, the more he had to wrestle with these negative forces.

One negative aspect that has come to the attention of journalists, photographers, and other media people who have reported on the Santo story is the line of defense—at times hostile—that has been drawn around the family. There appears to be an unwillingness to share Audrey's story with anyone whom the family fears may not publish a completely positive account. According to descriptions in the press and my own experience, Linda Santo is not eager to give access to people from the media whose motivations and sense of "Christian conscience," in her mind, are suspect. Linda made her suspicions of me very clear, in unfriendly tones that took me off guard as I had just come from an hour of serene contemplation in her chapel. In a lengthy feature on Audrey Santo, *Boston Phoenix* reporter Ellen Barry wrote: "To speak to Audrey Santo's family, journalists must be approved by her 'board of directors.' (The *Phoenix* was rejected by this body, whose taste runs to the Catholic press, and to reporters who guarantee previews of news copy.)"[8] In *Yankee* magazine, writer Edie Clark relayed that "journalists seeking the truth are first quizzed on their religious affiliations and whether or not their publications are 'spiritual.'" She added:

> I was told by the family spokesperson that Linda Santo "would not be available" for an interview. But while I was there, she was busy with reporters from television's "48 Hours," which does not, that I know of, have a spiritual inclination.[9]

These are a family's private decisions, of course, but Linda Santo's air of antagonism toward outsiders stands in stark contrast to the spiritual message she believes her daughter is destined to spread throughout the world. This falls into the category of the "shadow" aspect that Dr. Greene says is inevitable in a situation where a girl is being recognized as a specially chosen child of God.

In spite of these issues—from the projections that are possibly being placed on Audrey to the negativity experienced by some of the press and media—Dr. Greene believes that the Santo chapel can have a positive effect on visitors. "None of this necessarily nullifies the potential healing powers of the setting in which this girl is placed," he said. "The faithful, open-hearted, expectant trust with which people come for healing is a very real component in getting well. Doctors call it the placebo effect."

Looking at a spiritual dimension of the mind-body connection creates yet another framework in which to view the mysterious events surrounding Audrey Santo. Lionel Corbett, M.D., a Jungian analyst and author in California, describes the mind-matter connection as a continuum. Like a light spectrum, where blue is the invisible spirit/mind end and red is the visible physical/solid end, everything exists within the same system, he explains. Each point on the spectrum expresses a unique aspect of reality. The invisible aspects, such as thoughts, are no less "real" than the visible ones. In this continuum, a mystic's thoughts about the Passion of Christ are just as real as the stigmata that appear on his or her body. The physical manifestations exist on the dense end of the spectrum, while the mystic's devotional thoughts exist on the opposite, transparent end

An apparition of Mary appears on an unusual point on the spectrum, visible only to a visionary who is in touch with the Mother archetype, a fundamental "identity" that has been given different names throughout history. Archetypes are deep psychological structures that inform every part of human existence and are experienced by people across all cultures. "The archetype can be thought of as an . . . information source," Corbett writes in *The Religious Function of the Psyche*, "imagined as a strand of Big Mind, which informs the structure and function of both psyche and body." Psyche and body are not separate but part of one continuum—the body can be considered information "organized at a different density than psyche."[10] In this view of reality, the stigmata can be explained as the dense, physical manifestation of a transcendent reality expressing itself through the body. This logical framework is an extension of the mind-body connection that has become so significant in medicine. Describing the concept of the archetype further, Corbett writes:

> If we avoid thinking in terms of a body-psyche dualism, which seems to be only a perceptual artifact, there is no need to worry about how some non-physical source is linked to the body. . . . The archetype may become manifest both [mentally] as image or pattern, and also synchronistically as a body state such as an affect [emotion] or drive.[11]

Another "body state" would be the manifestation of the stigmata, as Audrey is reportedly experiencing. In *The Religious Function of the Psyche*, Corbett explores how contact with the archetypes brings on a numinous, or divine, experience. On the subject of spiritual experience, he explains, psychology and theology have been describing the same thing using different terminology. In his view, "elements of the divine are important in forming the very structure of the mind," and his method of therapy is actually an alternative approach to spirituality. Beneath the archetypes and the various images of divinity lies the unknowable mystery, the Creator. Like Jung, Corbett realizes that this is a realm beyond mind, beyond theories, and beyond our ability to speculate.

As in areas of hypnotism and mind-body medicine, Audrey's particular case poses unique challenges when proposing theories about the mind-body-spirit connection. Dr. Greene proposes that this connection is being revealed in the mysterious oil on the statues. They may be weeping to express the suffering that Audrey cannot communicate verbally, he suggests. Even though Audrey's cognitive abilities are very limited, if functioning at all, could she be communing with Jesus, as her mother claims, on a deeper level? If Audrey does not have the mental ability to contemplate God with words, even unspoken ones, could there be a deeper part of her consciousness that connects to the divine at some point on the body-psyche "spectrum" described by Dr. Corbett?

In *Healing Words: The Power of Prayer and the Practice of Medicine,* Larry Dossey, M.D., envisions a future in which the body, mind, and soul are recognized as aspects of one system. Like Corbett, he recognizes a religious aspect of the psyche and refers to it as the "nonlocal nature of consciousness." The nonlocal aspect of mind is not confined to the individual personality. Because the mind is not localized in the body but extends outside it, it is capable of affecting other bodies, even those far away. This is the framework in which Dr. Dossey discusses the power of prayer. Controlled scientific studies on patients have proved that prayer works, and *Healing Words* offers theories to explain how. Prayer, which was once considered simply a matter of faith, is now recognized among scientists and doctors as a valid, authentic force for healing. This is the beginning, Dr. Dossey hopes, of a greater understanding that takes the body-mind connection to a new level. "This soul-like quality of human beings," he writes, "will no longer be just an assertion of religions, to be accepted only through blind faith; it will be considered a legitimate implication of rational, empirical science."[12]

. . .

Joel S. Goldsmith (1892–1964), an American mystic and writer, viewed the stigmata as a product of the mind-body connection. He did not, however, believe that just thinking about God—even to the point that the marks of the Passion would appear on the body—was the real point of spirituality. In *Living by Grace* he explains that a thought about Christ, like a word about Christ, is not the same as the experience of Christ. "You can experience God, and you can experience Christ," he wrote, "but you can never know them aright with your mind." Regarding the stigmata, he continued:

> Many people in Europe each year experience on their bodies the wounds of the Master, and the world treats them as if they were mystics. They are not! They are emotional neurotics who live so intensely with the picture of the Passion in their minds that eventually the picture externalizes itself on their bodies. As a matter of fact, you can bring out anything you want on your body if you live inside with the feeling of it long enough, because the mind and the body (matter) are one, and whatever you take into your mind must manifest itself on your body.[13]

Goldsmith believed that the ultimate spiritual experience is achieved by quieting the mind and entering a meditative state in which one can listen for the "still, small Voice."

Thoughts are useless, he said, because "how could we possibly embrace the Allness of God with our little minds?"[14]

Modern stigmatic Padre Pio was accustomed to hearing psychological explanations for the stigmata he suffered for fifty years. Many people told him that they were not a miraculous gift from God but the result of his strong concentration on Christ and his Passion. In his typical brusque and witty style, he would often respond, "Go out to the fields and look very closely at a bull," he said. "Concentrate on him with all your might and see if you start to grow horns!"

Padre Pio's stigmata were examined by medical doctors many times throughout his life, and several physicians reported to the Vatican that they were not self-inflicted but were the result of unknown causes. After the friar's death, his Capuchin brothers began the long process of gathering data on the seemingly countless miracles attributed to him in his lifetime. They hoped that one day the pope would recognize Padre Pio's extraordinary holiness and declare him a saint. The investigation of miracles, like the road to sainthood, is long and complicated. It all starts at the local level, where a miraculous claim comes to the attention of the church. In Worcester, Massachusetts, reports of weeping crucifixes, bleeding Communion hosts, and miraculous claims of healing had caught the attention of the global press by the late 1980s. They had also caught the attention of the new local bishop, and an investigation was begun.

7.

Divine Scrutiny:
Investigating
a Miracle

Science without religion is lame, religion without science is blind.—Albert Einstein

"Every bishop dreads having one of these things happen in his diocese," Father Emmanuel McCarthy said of the Audrey Santo phenomenon. "It's hard to get an objective standpoint in an emotionally charged atmosphere."[1] When the Catholic Church investigates miracles, it approaches the issue with hard, rigorous skepticism. Believers sometimes take offense at this cold, businesslike attitude, but the church's reputation is at stake. False miracles, manufactured through fraud, delusion, mental illness, or other causes would mislead the faithful, and every measure is taken to rule them out.

By looking into the miracle, the local bishop is not trying to call attention to the event, as explained by Ray Delisle of Bishop Reilly's office: "The reason for doing an investigation is never to become a proponent of whatever is being claimed," he said. "Our goal isn't to put up a billboard saying, 'One more mile to Audrey's house.' We start from a point of skepticism. That is set."[2]

In this modern age of miracles, the Church has all the high-tech resources of twenty-first-century medicine and science at its disposal. The commission in Worcester is doing all it can to understand Audrey's condition, including her level of awareness (if any), as well as rule out any fraud in the appearance of oil and blood in the home. In the first phase of the investigation, which lasted fourteen months and was discussed in Bishop Reilly's public statement of January 1999, enough compelling material was discovered to bring the investigation to the next phase. According to Mary Cormier, spokesperson for the Santo family, this is the only investigation of a living person in the United States that has gone to this level.

During the first part of the investigation, the team studied prior analyses of the oil and conducted firsthand observations of the weeping images, including an overnight stay at the house. The bishop's investigatory commission consists of two psychologists, Dr. John Madonna and Dr. Robert Ciottone, and a theologian, Father Domenic Whedbe. Their initial investigation did not find any trickery, and during the overnight stay, even the small statue they brought with them began to weep oil. "Although we can't explain why oils and claims of blood are appearing on religious articles in the home," reported Bishop Reilly, "there is no obvious evidence of chicanery."

One of the most prevalent methods of fraud involving weeping statues is to use pig fat mixed with blood. As people enter the room and raise the air temperature, the fat mixture melts and blood appears on the image. The investigation did not uncover this type of fraud in the Santo home. In the new phase of the investigation, more tests are being conducted on the composition of the oil and the blood, as well as on Audrey's condition, as reported by Bishop Reilly:

> There is the need to have controlled tests performed involving some of the religious articles and lab analysis of resulting oils or other secretions since no two reports from past tests have come back with the same results. . . .
>
> The presence of oil is not proof, direct or indirect, of the miraculous. Paranormal activities in and of themselves, according to the perspective and practice of the Catholic Church, do not provide a basis for proving the miraculous. This has been the Church's confirmed directive for hundreds of years since Pope Benedict XIV (1740–58).
>
> When one applies fundamental rules of logic to the situation, even if the presence of the oil cannot be explained, one cannot presume that the inability to explain something automatically makes it miraculous. It certainly calls for scientific research and we will continue to do so.

Working with scientists at the UMass Memorial Medical Center in Worcester, the psychologists on the commission are developing tests to examine Audrey's cognitive and communicative abilities. Some tests will help them determine how much she responds to stimuli by measuring her pupil response and changes in her skin color and temperature. In his statement, Bishop Reilly explained the need for these tests:

> While family members claim that Audrey is able to communicate, there is no data to corroborate that claim from the available documentation of the medical professionals who have been involved in her care. With the family's cooperation, there is the need to perform specific testing using professionally accepted methods to determine brainwave activity when subjected to various external stimuli, for example the arrival and departure of family members from her room.

The investigators have set up time-lapse photography equipment to observe the statues in Audrey's bedroom that reportedly move on their own. They will also record everyone who comes into contact with Audrey to rule out an outside source of her stigmata. The commission has asked ABC's *20/20* to assist with some of the filming throughout this process.

During the first phase of the investigation, the bishop voiced concern about the number of people streaming through the home and filing past Audrey's window to get a look at her. After he discussed it with the family, the Santos stopped the bedroom-window visits and limited public access to the chapel in the garage. "She's getting a rest," Mary Cormier told *48 Hours*. "The bishop is very happy with that idea."[3]

Not all reports of miracles, apparitions, stigmata, and other supernatural events are investigated. The rare cases that do receive attention by the bishop may not get beyond the first phase when the investigation uncovers fraud or material that is not in line with Catholic teaching. A high-profile case that was rejected by a local bishop in recent years took place in Bayside in the borough of Queens, New York. Housewife and mother Veronica Lueken claimed to have received messages from Jesus, Mary, and various saints from 1970 until her death in 1995. She was instructed in her first vision to organize prayer vigils on the grounds of St. Robert Bellarmine Church in Bayside and to share with the world the heavenly messages she would regularly receive there. Mrs. Lueken's apparitions drew thousands of pilgrims, priests as well as laypeople, and the site came to be known as Our Lady of the Roses shrine. Claims of healings, conversions, and miraculous photographs of the Virgin Mary have been attributed to the site, which has since moved within Queens but is still very popular years after the visionary's death.

Mrs. Lueken, called "the Seer of Bayside," received hundreds of messages over more than three decades, some of which proclaimed that the Catholic Church was under the influence of evil forces. For example, a message reportedly given by the Virgin Mary on May 15, 1976, spoke out against the reforms of the Second Vatican Council (Vatican II):

> I repeat, My children, as I have told you in the past, that the great Council of Vatican II was manipulated by Satan. He sat there among you and he worked you like a chessboard. What can you do now to recover? It is simple, My children: turn back and start over with

the foundation given to you. You must bring respect
back to your priesthood.[4]

Another hotly controversial message proclaimed that an
"impostor" pope had governed the Church in place of Pope
Paul VI, who led the church from 1963 to 1978 and initiated many of the reforms of Vatican II, such as easing regu-
lations on interfaith marriages. In light of these messages,
Bishop Francis J. Mugavero of Brooklyn released a statement
in 1986 in which he maintained that the visions "completely
lacked authenticity." He specifically cited the message about
the impostor pope, stating that this type of "propaganda"
ran contrary to the teachings of the Church and instilled
doubts in the minds of the faithful. Bishop Mugavero's statement expressed his concern that the movement posed a
threat to the faith of the people who attended the vigils and
read the messages. "Anyone promoting this devotion," he
warned,

> is contributing to the confusion which is being created
> in the faith of God's people, as well as encouraging
> them to act against the determinations made by the le-
> gitimate pastor of this particular Church.
> It remains my constant hope that all the faithful
> spend their time and energies in promoting devotion
> to our Blessed Lady, in the many forms which have
> been approved by the Catholic Church.[5]

The Vatican department that is responsible for investigating candidates for sainthood is the Congregation for the

Causes of Saints. The first step is to establish whether the person lived a life of "heroic virtue," which makes him or her "venerable." Then a new set of criteria must be met to beatify, or make "blessed." The third and final step is to canonize the individual, declaring him or her a saint. Two miracles are required for beatification and two additional miracles for sainthood. If the cause is for a person who was martyred, the requirement of two miracles for beatification is dropped. Recent popes have decided that the ultimate sacrifice of one's life is sufficient. However, two authentic miracles must be approved for the martyr to become a saint.

Traditionally, the process of taking up a cause for sainthood is not begun until several years after the pious person's death. This gives time for the enthusiasm surrounding the individual to settle and for bias and prejudice to subside. If the person enjoyed a wide reputation for holiness in his or her lifetime, the cause may be taken up more quickly. When a person is made a saint, the church declares that he or she lives in glory in heaven with God. Sainthood is therefore a title conferred upon the dead, not the living. As Kenneth L. Woodward explains in *Making Saints*, "a 'living saint' is, canonically speaking, a contradiction in terms." He continues:

> Canonization takes place through a solemn papal declaration that a person is, for certain, with God. Because of that certainty, the faithful can, with confidence, pray to the saint to intercede with God on their behalf.[6]

The person at the Vatican responsible for verifying that cures are scientifically inexplicable is Dr. Raffaello Cortesini, chief of surgery at the University of Rome Medical School. As president of the Consulta Media, the official panel that investigates the medical cures, he has the final say on whether or not a claim is authentic. From October through July the panel meets every other week to examine two potential miracles. Almost 100 percent of the cases submitted are medical cures, and the documentation includes reports from hospitals, physicians, and nurses; the patient's full medical record; slides and biopsies or other physical evidence; written testimonies of the witnesses and the patient; and more. Each member of the panel spends many hours studying the material, and the bimonthly meetings are devoted to discussion and voting. The panel does not determine whether the cure is a miracle; that judgment is reserved for theologians in the Vatican. Dr. Cortesini submits a report on cures that he concludes cannot be attributed to medical science.

For hundreds of years a major part of the process toward sainthood was a court proceeding with representatives of the candidate on one side and a representative for the pope on the other. The pope's official was called the Promoter of the Faith, or more popularly, the Devil's Advocate, whose job was to challenge every piece of evidence. In this system an exhaustive trial-like proceeding exposed every minute detail of a case. In 1983 Pope John Paul II made sweeping reforms to the process, including eliminating the role of the Devil's Advocate. These changes were made in an effort to streamline and modernize the process. "No longer would the church look to the courtroom as its model for arriving at the truth," writes Woodward; "instead, it would employ the academic model of researching and writing a doctoral dissertation."[7]

Linda Santo is carefully filing the letters that come from those who claim to have been healed through Audrey's intercession. She is keeping detailed records of Audrey's stigmata, the symptoms that seem to replicate those of her visitors, and the bleeding Communion hosts and weeping statues. One day these records may be central to an even larger investigation into Audrey by the Catholic Church. After her death, whenever that may be, perhaps the Catholic Church will continue its investigation into the mysterious events that surrounded Audrey in life, and track down irrefutable proof that the healings attributed to her were authentic.

When the Church declares that an event is miraculous, it does not require that the faithful believe in the miracle. On the other hand, some Catholics, side by side with people of many different faiths, believe in miracles that have not been given the stamp of approval by the Church. Others don't give consideration to religious institutions at all but define the miraculous through their own eyes.

Thousands of people have waited in lines, crowded onto stadium bleachers, and traveled across the country to be near a girl who appears to be living a miracle. She came back to life after drowning, continues to live years beyond medical expectations, survived a cluster of cardiac arrests in a remote part of the world, and opens her eyes every morning.

The mysteries of sixteen-year-old Audrey Santo unfold around her and ripple out into the world. Safe in the care of a loving family, she speaks silently of hope and compassion and life. The next chapter in her story may be a remarkable discovery by her investigators or a glorious awakening in her sun-filled room. Or it may be a newfound peace in the heart of those who, seeing Audrey at church on her Anniversary Day, know they've seen a miracle.

. . .

In the front bedroom at 64 South Flagg Street, cameras roll while a nurse suctions Audrey's mouth and a medical researcher adjusts the electrodes on the girl's arm. The pleasant chatting of women drifts in from the kitchen, mingling with the rhythmic whoosh of a ventilator. On the other side of the house a visitor leans toward the chapel altar to look closely at a bloodstained Communion host displayed in an ornate golden reliquary. A priest who has just finished saying a short novena sits on a folding chair by the wall with his eyes closed. It's one-thirty on Thursday, and the chapel will close soon.

Down the block a man parks his van on Pleasant Street and opens the sliding door. His wife and four children, one of whom wears a complicated back brace, step out onto the curb. They see another man get out of his car just ahead, and ask, "Do you think they'll let us see the girl?"

A drop of oil falls from the chin of a statue of the Blessed Virgin Mary in the Santo chapel. In its first report about the investigation into the phenomena occurring in the Santo home, the Catholic diocese of Worcester, Massachusetts, stated that there is "no obvious evidence of chicanery" in the manifestation of the oil. (DAYNA SMITH © 1998, *THE WASHINGTON POST.* REPRINTED WITH PERMISSION.)

Appendix

January 1999 Statement by the Most
Reverend Daniel P. Reilly, Bishop of Worcester
and Diocese of Worcester Summary Report

Over the past eleven years, many unexplainable circumstances
have occurred around an innocent, bed-ridden girl named
Audrey Santo. In cooperation with the family, I have asked a
team of esteemed medical and theological professionals to review the situation to determine its possible impact, negative
or positive, on the family and the Catholic faithful.

After a year of careful planning and evaluation, the commission has reported its preliminary findings to me. A summary of those findings is available to anyone who requests
them, but I want to share some specific thoughts and concerns at this time as Bishop of the Diocese of Worcester.

The most striking evidence of the presence of God in the Santo home is seen in the dedication of the family to Audrey. Their constant respect for her dignity as a child of God is a poignant reminder that God touches our lives through the love and devotion of others.

There are inexplicable manifestations of oils and other substances emanating from religious objects in the Santo home. They are still under study. The purpose of the Church's investigation is not simply to become a promoter of claims of the miraculous. Rather, it is to review the theological foundations for such claims to assure that the faithful who follow them are not being misled.

In the case of Audrey herself, more study is needed from medical and other professionals regarding her level of awareness and her ability to communicate with the people around her. This is critical to the basis of the claim of her ability to intercede with God. In the meantime, I urge continued prayers *for* Audrey and her family. But praying *to* Audrey is not acceptable in Catholic teaching.

We are not yet able to confirm claims of miraculous events occurring at Audrey's home or as a result of a visit to Audrey, or from the oils associated with her. One need not make a personal visit to the Santo home. Indeed, continued demand for personal visitation poses the risk of compromising the family's ability to continue to offer excellent care to their daughter.

Further study has also been recommended and approved by me regarding the composition and source of the oils and other substances. In doing this, I want to underscore that any paranormal occurrences are not miraculous in and of themselves. The consistent practice of the Catholic Church has been not to use such occurrences as verifications of miraculous claims.

Finally, more systematic study must be done before the Church can even begin to evaluate the concept of "victim soul," which has been applied to Audrey. We must proceed quite cautiously here, since this term is not commonly used by the Church except for Christ himself who became the victim for our sins and transgressions on the cross.

While further study is being conducted, please pray for Audrey, for her family and for all those seeking healing and hope. I also ask for prayers to assist us so that this continued investigation will strengthen our faith in God's divine mercy and love.

SUMMARY REPORT

Introduction

The commission named by Bishop Reilly has completed its first phase of investigation of the extraordinary claims resulting from occurrences surrounding Audrey Santo, a young girl who has been in her family's care since an accidental near drowning eleven years ago. After developing a systematic method for investigation, the commission in this phase had as its objective the analysis of existing documents and materials as well as first hand witnessing of some of the "other than normal" experiences which were occurring at the home.

What was the focus of the commission?

The commission was responsible for developing a methodology for investigation consistent with Catholic teaching on these matters. It included the following four areas:

(1) Explanation of "paranormal" occurrences in the Santo home, namely the emitting of oils from statues and other religious objects and the presence of red stains which some say look like blood on four consecrated hosts.

(2) The ability of Audrey to communicate, at least to recognize the presence of others around her and to comprehend what is being said to her.

(3) The response of the family as it deals with this demanding situation regarding their youngest child, the paranormal activities occurring in the house and the requests by increasingly larger numbers of outsiders to visit Audrey.

Specifically,

Is the family or someone else causing the paranormal activities to occur through some form of chicanery?

What is the quality of the family's general care and concern for their daughter?

Does the family attempt to exploit interest in their situation for financial gain?

Does the family seek notoriety from the situation?

Does the family in any way seek to manipulate those who visit in order to direct their interpretation of the situation?

(4) The basis for the theological interpretations surrounding the claims, including

160

Are there miracles occurring that can be attributed directly to Audrey?

Is Audrey capable of being a victim soul, a title attributed to her by some people?

Are the claims being made in keeping with Catholic teaching?

Are the daily religious rituals and practices being performed according to approved liturgical practice?

Are the Catholic faithful at risk from anything when they visit the home or read materials from the Apostolate, which reports on Audrey, or view videotapes about Audrey? Is there the potential of a "cult" forming outside the control of the family or the Apostolate?

How does the Church explain the appearance of oils, blood, and other paranormal activities?

Although we can't explain why oils and claims of blood are appearing on religious articles in the home, there is no obvious evidence of chicanery. There is the need to have controlled tests performed involving some of the religious articles and lab analysis of resulting oils or other secretions since no two reports from past tests have come back with the same results.

Is the presence of this "mysterious" oil significant?

The presence of oil is not proof, direct or indirect, of the miraculous. Paranormal activities in and of themselves, according to the perspective and practice of the Catholic

Church, do not provide a basis for proving the miraculous. This has been the Church's confirmed directive for hundreds of years since Pope Benedict XIV (1740–58).

When one applies fundamental rules of logic to the situation, even if the presence of the oil cannot be explained, one cannot presume that the inability to explain something automatically makes it miraculous. It certainly calls for scientific research and we will continue to do so.

We must be careful not to identify this oil as "holy oil," which could be used to anoint a person. The Sacrament of the Anointing of the Sick, which can only be celebrated by a priest or bishop, uses oil blessed by the bishop at the Mass of Chrism, and is given to those who are seriously ill. This oil is properly called "oil of the sick." Additionally, an anointing by a priest or a bishop may be celebrated as part of a Eucharistic Liturgy for those who are ill, using oil blessed following the Rite of Anointing and Pastoral Care of the Sick.

The Church is responsible for determining the essential elements for the celebration of sacraments and how they are to be administered. Church law calls for pure olive oil or other plant oil to be used in the celebration of the sacrament. Consequently, the Church maintains that this "mysterious oil" should not be used in anointing a person who is ill.

Can Audrey communicate?

While family members claim that Audrey is able to communicate, there is no data to corroborate that claim from the available documentation of the medical professionals who have been involved in her care. With the family's cooperation, there is the need to perform specific testing using professionally accepted methods to determine brainwave activity when subjected to various external stimuli, for example the arrival and departure of family members from her room.

How has the family been responding, from the Church's perspective?

The family's constant love and devotion to their daughter is a miracle in the broad sense of the word. They have always recognized the human dignity of their daughter, despite the circumstances. And, they never cease to open up the door to their home as well as their hearts to the needs of the suffering who write to them and call upon them each day.

More than anything else, those who visit the family make note of the excellent care the family gives to their daughter. This has manifested itself in her physical condition, for example, she has not apparently had bedsores in the eleven years she has been confined to her bed.

Does the family seek financial gain from the situation?

There is no evidence that the family has sought financial gain for themselves. On the contrary, they have not sold the oil which appears in their home and the Apostolate request only nominal donations for videotapes and other materials about Audrey. These donations are used to assist the Apostolate in the costs incurred to correspond with those who have written to Audrey and to publish a periodic newsletter about Audrey.

Notoriety is of some concern. The family does not seek it for themselves but they certainly do so for Audrey. This has led some people to expect intercessions from Audrey and/or miracles long before anyone has had a chance to evaluate these claims more thoroughly. It has also put the family in a more awkward position of having far more demand for personal visits than it can ever accommodate, while continuing to offer excellent care for their daughter.

Are visitors manipulated in order to experience certain things?

Staged or planned manipulation of the visitors to the house is not apparent. The general attitude in the house is friendly, warm and inviting without any sanctimony or undue reverence. However, it must be pointed out that the groups arriving together as they do, often tend to share certain characteristics in facing terminal illness (their own or that of a loved one) or, at least, tend to be far from skeptical regarding the possibility of experiencing a miracle.

Is the Church ready to say one way or another if miracles attributed to Audrey are occurring?

It will take significant time and resources to determine if miracles are directly attributable to Audrey. Many of the cases cited publicly concerning Audrey's intercession have had medical opinions, which did not rule out the potential for normal recovery (in whole or in part). Before any objective investigation can be done directly on this question, issues such as Audrey's level of consciousness and ability to communicate need to be corroborated (see above request for further testing). There will also be the need to set up a clearing-house involving medical authorities to review specific claims of physical cures.

Is Audrey a Victim Soul?

The term "victim soul" is not an official term in the Church. It was used in some circles in the 18th and 19th century when there was a fascination with suffering and death, in an attempt to offer the possibility that one person could suffer for another. Christians believe that Jesus is the sacrificial lamb, the victim for our sins. His suffering and death redeemed humanity from sin and eternal death. Through baptism we share in Christ's death with the hope that we will share in his resurrection, his glory. To begin to consider this notion of "victim soul" with regards to Audrey, one would have to establish a corroborated understanding of Audrey's cognitive abilities. This has yet to be done. Beyond that, one would have to determine that Audrey, at the age of three was, and presently is, capable of making a free choice to accept the suffering of others.

Are there practices at the family's home which are contrary to acceptable Catholic rituals?

Fidelity to the sacraments and to approved liturgical rituals has been noted. Specific areas of concern, such that they should be discontinued regardless of the outcome of this investigation, are as follows:

(1) One should only pray *for* Audrey. Our faith teaches us to pray to God and to pray for the intercession of the saints. Therefore, the distribution of a "Prayer to Audrey" should cease immediately.

(2) Whether or not claims of blood are proven to be present on the consecrated Eucharist in the tabernacle in the home, it must be presented in the

context that the transubstantiation we witness at every celebration of the Eucharist is the same. There should be no implications that hosts consecrated at Mass in the Santo home are "better" or even unique. When used in Benediction or Exposition, only one consecrated host should be used, in keeping with approved liturgical practice.

Are there any priests officially assigned as chaplains or spiritual directors to Audrey?
No. Priests who are involved with the family are acting on their own behalf in personally working with the family. Audrey and her family are members of Christ the King parish. The pastor of Christ the King is responsive to and available for their spiritual needs.

Is the investigation over?
The first phase of the investigation, which was to compare existing reports for possible corroboration, is complete. Additional quantifiable study is needed, as cited above in this document, in order to attempt to define the composition of the oil and to verify other claims, as well as to determine Audrey's ability to recognize and respond to outside stimuli. Those tests need to be done before determining whether further theological investigation is warranted.

Bibliography

BOOKS

Adams, Henry. *Mont Saint Michel and Chartres.* New York: Penguin Books, 1986.

Ariès, Philippe and Georges Duby, general editors. *A History of Private Life: Revelations of the Medieval World.* Cambridge: Harvard University Press, 1988.

Catechism of the Catholic Church. New York: Doubleday, 1995.

Corbett, Lionel, M.D. *The Religious Function of the Psyche.* London: Routledge, 1996.

Delaney, John J. *Pocket Dictionary of Saints,* Abridged ed. New York: Image, 1983.

Dossey, Larry, M.D. *Healing Words: The Power of Prayer and the Practice of Medicine.* San Francisco: HarperSanFrancisco, 1993.

———. *Meaning and Medicine: Lessons from a Doctor's Tales of Breakthrough and Healing.* New York: Bantam Books, 1992.

Freze, Michael, S.F.O. *They Bore the Wounds of Christ: The Mystery of the Sacred Stigmata.* Huntington, Ind.: Our Sunday Visitor, 1989.

Goldsmith, Joel S. *Living by Grace.* San Francisco: HarperSanFrancisco, 1992.

Hardon, John A., S.J. *Pocket Catholic Dictionary*. New York: Doubleday, 1985.

Harrison, Ted. *Stigmata: A Medieval Mystery in a Modern Age*. New York: Penguin Books, 1996.

Herbstrith, Waltraud. *Edith Stein: A Biography: The Untold Story of the Philosopher and Mystic Who Lost Her Life in the Death Camps of Auschwitz*. San Francisco: Harper & Row, 1985.

Institute of Noetic Sciences with William Poole. *The Heart of Healing*. Atlanta: Turner Publishing, 1993.

James, William. *The Varieties of Religious Experience*. New York: Penguin Books, 1985.

Johnson, Kevin Orlin, Ph.D. *Apparitions: Mystic Phenomena and What They Mean*. Dallas: Pangaeus Press, 1998.

Johnson, Maxwell E. *The Rites of Christian Initiation: Their Evolution and Interpretation*. Collegeville, Minn.: Liturgical Press, 1999.

Jung, Carl G. *The Collected Works of C. G. Jung*, Volume 9: *The Archetypes and the Collective Unconscious*, Second edition. Translated by R.F.C. Hull. Princeton, N.J.: Princeton University Press (Bollingen Series XX), 1968.

Lewis, C. W. *Miracles*. New York: Simon & Schuster, 1996.

Mechthild von Magdeburg. *The Flowing Light of the Godhead*. Translated by Frank Tobin. New York: Paulist Press, 1998.

Nickell, Joe. *Looking for a Miracle: Weeping Icons, Relics, Stigmata, Visions, and Healing Cures*. Buffalo, N.Y. Prometheus Books, 1993.

O'Brien, Elmer, S.J. *Varieties of Mystic Experience*. New York: Holt, Rinehart and Winston, 1964.

Pelletier, Joseph A., A.A. *The Sun Danced at Fatima*. Garden City, N.Y.: Image, 1983.

Petrisko, Thomas A. *In God's Hands: The Miraculous Story of Little Audrey Santo*. McKees Rocks, Pa.: St. Andrew's Productions, 1997.

Pope John Paul II. *Crossing the Threshold of Hope*. New York: Alfred A. Knopf, 1994.

———. *Gift and Mystery: On the Fiftieth Anniversary of My Priestly Ordination*. New York: Doubleday, 1996.

Ruffin, C. Bernard. *Padre Pio: The True Story*. Huntington, Ind.: Our Sunday Visitor, 1991.

Teresa of Ávila, Saint. *The Life of Saint Teresa of Ávila by Herself*, translated by J. M. Cohen. New York: Penguin Books, 1957.

Thomas à Kempis. *The Imitation of Christ*. Translated by Richard Whitford. New York: Image, 1955.

von Franz, Marie-Louise. *Psyche and Matter*. Boston: Shambhala, 1992.

Wilson, Ian. *The Bleeding Mind: An Investigation into the Mysterious Phenomenon of Stigmata.* London: Weidenfeld and Nicolson, 1988.

Woodward, Kenneth L. *Making Saints: How the Catholic Church Determines Who Becomes a Saint, Who Doesn't, and Why.* New York: Touchstone/Simon & Schuster, 1996.

MEDIA

The Story of Little Audrey Santo. Worcester, Mass.: Apostolate of a Silent Soul, 1997. Video.

Audrey's Life: Voice of a Silent Soul. Mundelein, Ill.: The Mercy Foundation, 1996. Video.

"Faithful to Audrey." *48 Hours.* CBS. June 24, 1999. Burrelle's Information Service transcript.

"The Miracle of Audrey." *20/20.* ABC. May 31, 1999. Author's television transcript.

Pilgrimage to Audrey Santo. Father Leroy Smith. Cincinnati: Our Lady of the Holy Spirit Center, 1996. Audiotape transcript.

Notes

1: INTENSIVE CARE

1. *Audrey's Life: Voice of a Silent Soul,* video.
2. Ibid.
3. *Worcester Telegram & Gazette,* August 10, 1987.
4. Ibid.
5. Ibid., October 11, 1987.
6. Ibid., August 10, 1987.
7. Ibid., October 11, 1987.
8. *The Story of Little Audrey Santo,* video.
9. *Worcester Telegram & Gazette,* October 11, 1987.
10. Ibid., January 8, 1988.
11. "The Miracle of Audrey," *20/20* (ABC, May 31, 1999).
12. "Faithful to Audrey," *48 Hours* (CBS, June 24, 1999).
13. *Audrey's Life: Voice of a Silent Soul.*
14. *Worcester Telegram & Gazette,* November 14, 1987.

15. Ibid., January 8, 1988.
16. *Catechism of the Catholic Church,* paragraphs 2674, 2679, 2683, and 2558.

2: A MOTHER'S MISSION

1. Michael Freze, *They Bore the Wounds of Christ,* p. 268.
2. *Washington Post,* July 19, 1998.
3. *48 Hours.*
4. Newsletter of the Apostolate of a Silent Soul, Inc. vol. 2, no. 11 (November 1999).
5. Ibid.
6. Ibid.
7. *Washington Post,* July 19, 1998.
8. Thomas W. Petrisko, *In God's Hands: The Miraculous Story of Little Audrey Santo,* p. 19.
9. Ibid.
10. John A. Hardon, *Pocket Catholic Dictionary,* p. 110.
11. *Boston Globe,* September 1897, courtesy of the Roxbury Carmelite Monastery Library.
12. Saint Teresa of Ávila, *The Life of Saint Teresa of Ávila by Herself,* translated by J. M. Cohen, p. 93.
13. Brochure of the Carmelite Monastery, Roxbury, Massachusetts.
14. Petrisko, p. 20.
15. *The Story of Little Audrey Santo.*
16. Petrisko, p. 204.
17. *Worcester Sunday Telegram,* January 30, 2000.
18. Ibid., January 20, 2000.
19. Superior Court records, Commonwealth of Massachusetts.

20. *Worcester Sunday Telegram,* January 20, 2000.

21. *Washington Post,* July 19, 1998.

22. Transcript of Ivan Dragicevic's talk at Shorline Center Auditorium in Seattle, Washington, on October 29, 1997, as posted on www. medjugorje.org/ivan2.htm.

23. Henry Adams, *Mont Saint Michel and Chartres,* p. 248.

24. Ibid., pp. 92–93.

25. Ibid., pp. 92, 96.

26. Lionel Corbett, *The Religious Function of the Psyche,* p. 77.

27. Posted on the Marian Library/International Marian Research Institute Web site (www.udayton.edu/mary).

28. G. Scott Sparrow, Ed.D., *Blessed Among Women: Encounters with Mary and Her Message* (New York: Three Rivers Press, 1997), pp. 2, 258.

29. *Worcester Telegram & Gazette,* July 12, 1988.

30. *Washington Post,* July 19, 1998.

31. Petrisko, p. 49.

32. *Worcester Telegram & Gazette,* August 6, 1988.

33. Ibid.

34. Ibid., September 12, 1988.

35. Ibid.

3: STIGMATA: THE SACRED WOUNDS

1. C. Bernard Ruffin, *Padre Pio: The True Story,* p. 155.

2. Petrisko, pp. 97, 98.

3. *Washington Post,* July 19, 1998.

4. *New Orleans Times-Picayune,* February 6, 1999.

5. *Washington Post,* July 19, 1998.

6. Petrisko, p. 101.
7. *The Catholic Encyclopedia,* vol. 14 (Robert Appleton Company, 1913, on-line edition © 1999 by Kevin Knight).
8. *The New Catholic Encyclopedia,* vol. 13 (New York: McGraw-Hill, 1967).
9. Posted on the Web site www.CWNews.com (Catholic World News), May 3, 1999.
10. Thomas à Kempis, *The Imitation of Christ,* translated by Richard Whitford, p. 76.
11. Philippe Braunstein, "Toward Intimacy: The Fourteenth and Fifteenth Centuries," in *A History of Private Life: Revelations of the Medieval World,* p. 626.
12. Ibid.
13. *New Catholic Encyclopedia,* vol. 13.
14. Ian Wilson, *The Bleeding Mind,* p. 99.
15. Johannes Jørgensen, *Saint Francis of Assisi* (New York: Doubleday, 1911), p. 247.
16. Ibid., p. 248.
17. Saint Teresa of Ávila, *Book of Her Life,* as quoted in *Apparitions: Mystic Phenomena and What They Mean* by Kevin Orlin Johnson, p. 48.
18. Anne Emmerich, as quoted in *Ecstatic Confessions* by Martin Buber (San Francisco: Harper & Row, 1985), p. 138.
19. Ibid., p. 136.
20. Ruffin, p. 152.
21. Ibid., p. 261.
22. Ibid., p. 161.
23. Posted on www.CWNews.com, May 3, 1999.
24. FIDES (Vatican news service), as posted on www.CWNews.com, April 30, 1999.

25. Vatican Decree on the Heroic Virtues of Venerable Padre Pio, posted on www.ncfpp.com.
26. Christina Gallagher, as posted on her official Web site at web.frontier.net/cgallagher.
27. Ibid.
28. Statement posted on the Web site www.smcenter.org/najuweb.htm.
29. From an interview posted on the Web site www.greatcrusade.org.
30. *Washington Post,* April 5, 1992.
31. Ibid., August 18, 1997.
32. Petrisko, p. 94.
33. *Audrey's Life: Voice of a Silent Soul.*
34. *The Story of Little Audrey Santo.*
35. Petrisko, p. 71.
36. Ibid., p. 100.

4: STRANGE PATHS: THE SUFFERER AND VICTIM SOUL

1. Mechthild of Magdeburg, *The Flowing Light of the Godhead,* trans. by Frank Tobin, p. 52.
2. Johnson, p. 85.
3. Mechthild of Magdeburg, p. 181.
4. Buber, p. 82.
5. Saint Teresa of Ávila, *The Interior Castle,* as quoted in Elmer O'Brien, *Varieties of Mystic Experience,* p. 273.
6. Colossians 1:24–25
7. *Interior Castle,* p. 45.
8. John J. Delaney, *Pocket Dictionary of Saints,* p. 325.
9. Ruffin, p. 151.
10. Ibid.

11. Waltraud Herbstrith, *Edith Stein: A Biography*, pp. 94–95.
12. Ibid., p. 95.
13. Quoted on CWNews service, October 12, 1998.
14. Quoted on Gallagher's Web site: web.frontier.net/cgallagher.
15. Worcester diocese summary report (see Index).
16. Petrisko, p. 181.
17. *20/20.*
18. Petrisko, p. 96.
19. *The Story of Little Audrey Santo.*
20. Ibid.
21. Ibid.
22. *Audrey's Life: Voice of a Silent Soul.*
23. *The Story of Little Audrey Santo.*
24. Petrisko, p. 169.
25. Ibid.
26. William James, *The Varieties of Religious Experience*, p. 362.
27. Pope John Paul II, *Crossing the Threshold of Hope*, p. 64.
28. Ibid., pp. 60–66.
29. Ibid., p. 25.
30. *Catechism of the Catholic Church*, p. 423.
31. Ibid., p. 417.
32. Posted on the Web site www.melkite.org/Stein2.html.
33. *The Story of Little Audrey Santo.*
34. Petrisko, p. 145.
35. Ibid.
36. *The Story of Little Audrey Santo.*

5: MIRACLES ON FLAGG STREET

1. *48 Hours.*

2. Edie Clark, "Audrey's Story: Love's Power to Heal," *Yankee*, February 2000.

3. *Audrey's Life: Voice of a Silent Soul.*

4. Ibid.

5. *20/20.*

6. Posted on the Web site www.melkite.org/Stein2.html.

7. *Catechism of the Catholic Church*, p. 200.

8. Maxwell E. Johnson, *The Rites of Christian Initiation*, pp. 30–31.

9. Ibid., pp. 115–116.

10. Ibid., pp. 131–132.

11. *Pilgrimage to Audrey Santo*, audiotape transcript.

12. "Audrey Santo: A Priest Meets a Victim Soul" as posted on the National Catholic Network, www.ncn.net (site no longer available).

13. *Audrey's Life: Voice of a Silent Soul.*

14. Pope John Paul II, *Gift and Mystery*, p. 75.

15. Statement released by the Eparchy of Toronto Apostolic Administrator Chancery Office, posted on www.frontier.net/Apparitions/Naju.ch.html.bishop.

16. *The Story of Little Audrey Santo.*

17. *48 Hours.*

18. *Worcester Telegram & Gazette*, January 30, 2000.

19. *The Story of Little Audrey Santo.*

20. *Pilgrimage to Audrey Santo.*

21. Ted Harrison, *Stigmata*, p. 85.

22. Geoffrey Parrinder, *Mysticism in the World's Religions* (Oxford: Oneworld Publications, 1997), p. 195.

6: MIRACLES OR MIND POWER?

1. *48 Hours.*
2. *Boston Globe,* January 22, 1999.
3. Larry Dossey, *Meaning and Medicine,* pp. 20–21.
4. Wilson, p. 97.
5. *Worcester Telegram & Gazette,* January 30, 2000.
6. Harrison, p. 17.
7. Marie-Louise von Franz, *Psyche and Matter,* p. 160.
8. *Boston Phoenix,* December 29, 1997.
9. *Yankee,* February 2000.
10. Corbett, p. 58.
11. Ibid.
12. Larry Dossey, *Healing Words,* p. 206.
13. Joel S. Goldsmith, *Living by Grace,* p. 70.
14. Ibid., p. 71.

7: DIVINE SCRUTINY: INVESTIGATING A MIRACLE

1. *Boston Phoenix,* December 29, 1997.
2. *Chicago Tribune,* March 23, 1999.
3. *48 Hours.*
4. Posted on the Our Lady of the Roses shrine Web site, www.roses.org.
5. Posted on the Web site www.ewtn.com, courtesy of the Catholic Resource Network.
6. Kenneth L. Woodward, *Making Saints,* p. 17.
7. Ibid., p. 91.

If you would like to contact Audrey Santo's volunteer organization
to request oil or subscribe to the newsletter, write to:

The Apostolate of a Silent Soul, Inc.
West Side Station
P.O. Box 746
Worcester, MA 01602